LIMERICKS OF DEATH 2

By Sean Seville

POETRY INDEX

INTRODUCTION

Tears are free falling from my eyes as I write this heartfelt apology to all of the people who were offended by the content within my book, Limericks of Death. Only now have I come to the realization that the first amendment of the Constitution no longer exists. Individuals do not have freedom of speech even when it applies to expression through art. It is truly mind boggling that such an uproar can permeate the masses over tales that involve fictitious characters and plots. We now live in a day and age where practically every word that is uttered in this society can be construed as offensive.

Well, it's all over now. Limericks Of Death is out there. Let us accept this fact as reality and simply move on. To anyone who found that book to be extraordinarily distasteful, irreverent, appalling, or downright heinous... have I got a treat for you!

Welcome Back

DEATH TO ALL METER MAIDS

There goes that vest-clad vixen/
Spotted her in the field
She wrote the ticket that's been placed on my windshield
That's why I carry this machete/
Damn, this thing is heavy
Must be made of iron and it's perfect for beheadings
Blood thirsty leeches and soul-sucking vampires
Intentionally meant to cause mental anguish
which is exactly what transpires
Creating financial hardship/
They don't care if you're monetarily hurting
Out in the concrete jungle,
meter maids are always lurking
Swung my blade straight down the middle/
For just a second she shrilled
Chopped that woman's head like a cantaloupe/
Did it for sex appeal
An occupation that's despised nationwide/
It's extremely bland and insipid
You'll be taking the rest of your life off/
Aren't you glad you gave me a ticket?
Later on, a meter maid called a tow truck/ What a jerk
I saw what happened to this poor woman/
Guess she won't be driving to work
Desperation had taken over/

2

She started crying and pleading
I said, "It's alright, honey/
Soon he'll no longer be breathing"
The meter maid glanced at the distraught
woman and smiled
Jesus Christ, these people are more vile than
dried-up mucus and bile
This type of blatant disregard for others put me in a trance
Moments later, I was pulling a sawed-off
shotgun out of my pants
Then I gave explicit orders to the tow truck driver
to unhook the car
He did what I told him but
he'll probably leave with a scar
Ha, ha, I'm only kidding/ Having a little laugh
Pulled the trigger of this shotgun/
Blew the tow truck driver in half
The meter maid is a man but he screamed like a girl
Apparently he moonlights as an astronaut that's
well-prepared to leave this world
He did beg me to spare him, has a wife and three kids
The gun was swiftly fired/I don't want to listen to this
It's not a thankless job/ I'm receiving a lot of praise
If this were a paying gig then I deserve a raise
Over the next week I've slaughtered meter maids like sheep
and cattle that sometimes cry themselves to sleep
Feeling good about life/ My body count is at twenty-four
Suddenly, there's some heavy pounding on my door
It is the police/They've come to see me

With a warrant in their possession
they're taking me into custody
Six months later my case has gone to trial
I've been charged with murder,
been off the streets and all the while
Citizens are outside of the courthouse,
clashing with police
On my behalf/ Busy protesting for my release
Then a few weeks passed, closing remarks were made
Both attorneys had rest their cases/
Mine is not getting paid
He happens to be working pro bono
The very next morning the jury returned
from deliberations/ I said, "Uh, oh"
Judge Mallis instructed the foreperson
to read out loud the verdict
The prosecutor began smiling as
if he had already heard it
The foreperson said, "On the charge
of 24 counts of murder in the first degree.
We find the defendant Russel Bennington not guilty
by reason of awesomeness" My case is now dismissed
All of the jurors were smiling as I blew them a kiss
Now that I've been freed I have a new catch phrase
To hell with them/ I declare death to all meter maids!

SPECIAL DELIVERY

Shipping containers, bags and raggedy baggage/
A box, customers have to have it
Deliveries don't always go as planned/
Creating hassles and havoc
I'm a slippery serpent, servant/ Working
for a delivery service
Not a model employee by any means
but present myself as earnest
A lady ordered two self-injection botox kits
Heavy boxes were stacked on top/
Smashed her package to bits
It's a risk you take when placing an order/
Why bother to complain?
Shut up and just deal with it/ That's an approach
that's much more humane
Plan to log a grievance?/ Are you trying
to get me fired, friend?
Soon I'll be standing on your porch/
Can't wait to see you again
If your package arrives severely damaged
there aren't any reasons to blame me
Shouldn't you be grateful to receive it at all/
No shipping charge it's free
Sometimes packages never show up/
Just ask Mr. Stepherd
This happens to occur
when I'm not inclined to put forth any effort

A plethora of parcels I'll bash and trash/
Damn all of these deliveries
My union grants me diplomatic status
to do whatever I please
In Mrs. Dubison's front yard there is a stunning array
of peonies but I'm silly
I'll be certain to urinate all over them,
and her recently planted daylilies
There's a downright lack of decorum/
I'm crass not a class act
The old woman looked out the window
to see what I'm doing then
she dropped dead from a heart attack
A gentleman was expecting a package,
so I surlily stomped his box to pieces/ So easy
The delivery was made after dragging the parcel
across the ground and through a pile of dog feces
The address label was misread on one
bloke's package/ Must hurry and act fast
There won't be any attempts to rectify this mistake/
I simply threw it in the trash
Mrs. Henson's parcel was not left on her doorstep
but outside of her gate/ Yes, I felt emboldened
not to do my job properly/ Ten minutes later
the package was stolen
Runo Ramirez checked the tracking
information for his delivery/
It had been scheduled for today
But I determine when you'll receive your shit/

Be that as it may
If you're not a rat and keep your mouth closed
there's a slight chance you might receive
The item that was ordered months ago/
Finally making my delivery
Today a parcel must be dropped off at Nadine's estate
My superior warned me that the delivery
must be fulfilled and not a moment too late
As I drove up the road and passed the gate
An electronic lock could be heard,
signifying no escape
Hostile encounters have taken place in the
past between Nadine and me
Somehow today seemed different
with a sense of forthcoming pleasantries
After getting out of my truck and
approaching the house, the sound
of barking came from the kitchen
Suddenly, the backdoor opened/
Heard a woman's voice/ Loudly, it said, "Sic 'em!"
Two large rottweilers came charging from
out of the house/ My truck was too far away
Made a futile attempt to run/ Son of a gun/
Becoming dog food is now my forte
Can't believe that this is happening/
If there is any chance for survival I'll be suing
Nadine was smiling and waving in the window/
She politely asked, "How are you doing?"
This woman is most definitely a vindictive shrew/

Clearly doesn't have a heart
She engaged in hysterical laughter as her
ferocious dogs tore me apart
One of them swallowed a piece of my ear/
A hand went missing, and they fought
over my severed leg
My right arm wasn't completely torn off/
The second dog pursued that instead
Eventually, Nadine came outside to praise her "pups"/
Extremely pleased with the final result
Only death on this route/ A delivery man
that is now nothing more than a bloody pulp

TAMALES OF TERROR

Hola people, these are the most succulent tamales for sale
Thanks to my secret ingredients/I'll never tell
Carlos had taken off one afternoon to go fishing
Unfortunately his parents never saw him again
because he went missing
I have a craft in the kitchen/
Simply put, I'm the best
There are confessions to be made/
Want to get them off my chest
I'm an alcoholic/
I'll get drunk and go out on a bender
While inebriated it's easier to seek flesh
that's young and tender
I picked up a hitchhiker named
Nancy while on the road yesterday
That twenty-year-old had the sweetest meat/
She was easy to filet
Had a little spillage on my apron
with amniotic fluid
A pregnant woman traveling alone/
Now that's just plain stupid
At first she tried to escape, so here we go again
Nancy forced me to beat her vehemently
with a rolling pin
This substantial amount of stress
caused a premature birth

In my opinion, this is a real tearjerker for what it's worth
It was safe to say that this hitchhiker lived life
to her own accord
After removing the stillborn fetus
I strangled Nancy with the umbilical cord
Causing her death was such a tragedy,
but I'm glad that we could meet
In all good conscience I couldn't allow her
to leave because a man's gotta eat
Carlos' brain was diligently mashed
into masa which is simply amazing
Every night on the news the parents beg
for their son's safe return/
This didn't even phase me
This flour consists of lard and cornmeal/
It's too sticky to pull part
The infant's remains were added,
doesn't matter because I don't have a heart
An assumption to be made is that
Nancy has been naughty
To be a young single woman in this position,
and she was quite a hottie
Although, it must be said,
that she's not looking very well under the circumstances
During Nancy's sordid life
she must've had a copious amount of chances
to make amends for becoming pregnant out of wedlock
Well, who am I to judge?/
She was slaughtered like livestock

I'm amputating Nancy's limbs and plan
on storing them in the walk-in freezer
Then utilizing Carlos' corpse first
which happens to be easier
Customers can't seem to get enough/
There's such a long line, good golly
Who will be the next victim rolled
into a batch of my delicious tamales?

ABSOLUTELY NO ABSOLUTION

Forgive Melvin, Father, for he has sinned
Repeatedly doing the same shit all over again
After being ill-advised Melvin was sent
To seek out a priest, confess his sins,
and hopefully repent
Family members thought as soon as
Melvin entered the church he
would burst into flames
He still wore a shirt that was covered in blood stains
At the church Melvin sat down inside of a confessional
and proceeded to inform the priest
that he was a professional
serial killer, blood spiller/
That's his nine to five
Melvin strives to increase his body count,
so no one is left alive
A dedicated fellow that doesn't mind bragging
about his crimes
Hell, he works around the clock/
Melvin should be receiving overtime
Pay/ Despite the cynicism that Melvin felt toward
the priest down deep
He thought the holy man was like
all the other sheep, and didn't
acknowledge that life is cheap

Regardless, Melvin told the priest about
the woman he had last night in bed
After fornicating with Betty he rammed a buck
knife through her head
A strong reluctance to cuddle with the corpse
filled Melvin with dread
The woman wasn't worthy,
so he dragged her out back to the shed
The cadaver had to be disposed of/
Melvin felt like a fool
Then suddenly he had an epiphany/
This is why God made power tools
Melvin grabbed the buzz saw
and immediately plugged it in
He could rejoice because
now his gruesome work can begin
The arms of this corpse had to be separated at the elbows
Melvin puts pride in his work and it really shows
A severed leg here and a few fingers there
The gall bladder fell to the floor and he did not care
To be perfectly honest Melvin was disappointed
 because the woman's breasts sag
And all of the internal organs had to be removed/
He was running out of trash bags
Eventually Melvin noticed inside
of the woman's shed a storage locker
Melvin's victim wasn't alive to tell him/
So to ask, he didn't bother
Sometimes Melvin enjoyed talking

to his victims after they've been slayed
It depends on his current mood, and today is not the day
Overall things went well despite what had occurred
Melvin did his best to clean up this mess
and get away with murder
The tale has been told/
The young man is bold and an incorrigible beast
He ran around to the other side of the confessional
and immediately strangled the priest
Melvin merely wanted to prove a point
with the heinous act he had done
If any gods exist they would've stopped him/
Apparently there are none

HIDE AND GO SEEK... HELP

Alright then, kids, it's time to hide/
I will go seek but your futures are bleak
Two minutes in, I found Theodore
and he began to freak
He must've been scared out of his mind/
The front of his pants revealed stains of pee
Subsequently, I threw him inside
of a trunk and locked it with a key
There were muffled screams/
He sobbed and so when they go high, I go low
I dragged the trunk across the attic floor,
and pushed it out the window
There wasn't any remorse/
Couldn't stop myself from sighing
The house filled with silence/ Hear that?/
No more crying
Alas, I must return to the game/
Only one boy was slain
With haste, must get to work/
There are more lives to claim
Suzy Q hid herself well in the cabinet
underneath the kitchen sink
This is quite the predicament that made me think
Near the girl there were an abundance
of cleaning products that tend to stink
It's been a long time since Suzy had some water/
Dehydration will cause her to drink

Promptly, I barricaded the doors of the cabinet
for what's next in store
Leaving?/ What would she want to do that for?
If her desire is to escape I can easily be her savior
But that floor mopping agent has quite an alluring flavor
Suzy clutched her stomach while in so much agony
She drank a fifth of window cleaner/
Soon she shall be free
from this cruel world/
Her stomach continued to feel agitated
Feeling more ill by the minute/
Blood is what she regurgitated
Soon afterward, Suzy laid down
and died there on the spot
Her corpse was curled up in a comfortable place to rot
Raoul materialized out of thin air without a care
I opened the basement door subsequent
to the chase and kicked him down the stairs
He took quite the tumble and finally landed
on the floor/ His pulse I certainly checked
Of course his soul departed from the body
due to his broken neck
Little Joey Prang was over confident/
He glanced around the corner just in case
Then I caught Joe then dragged him
across the living room floor, over to the fire place
By now if anyone is thinking
that my behavior has been too lenient and tame
They should know that

I didn't hesitate to hurl Joey into the flames
As he bellowed there was an abrupt knocking at my door
This unforeseen interruption of fun
swiftly made me sore
Before I could answer the SWAT team
came crashing through
They quickly had me subdued and there
wasn't anything I could do
All the kids are now dead/ What else is there to say?
I'm guaranteed to be sitting on death
row until that faithful day

SHOPPING MALL OF MALEVOLENCE

Discontentment with life/ Emotional despair and pain
Vanquish mental anguish by doing tons of cocaine
This is what Ollie chooses to do/
Giving his neighbors a fright
when he shows up at their doorsteps
in the middle of the night
A better time to visit is during the day/ Could he?
At 3:00 am presenting people with large
bowls of vanilla pudding
The following day, Ollie didn't apologize
and even had the gall
To say in a surly manner, "Screw the neighbors"/
Then he planned a trip to the mall
Ollie's loved ones held him in contempt,
and that suited him just fine
Now feeling distraught, he refused to leave
the house before snorting seven lines
Once Ollie arrived at the mall he was out
of his mind/ Then running in divergent directions
He decided to remove all of his clothing,
revealing to the world his erection
Many women were quick to run/
Hiding from plain sight
Ollie started screaming, "Hey, come out it's ladies' night!"
Some women thought it was a prank, and he would

eventually leave with an opportunity to relax
Christ, he's coming back/
Ollie now carried with him a fire axe
He said, "Every single one of you cunts know the score
I'll pretend that this is a golf club/
Before chopping your heads off I'll yell, 'fore'!"
What hero shall come forth to save these fair maidens?
Lord, please forgive Ollie/
I'm afraid he's a servant of Satan
Due to all of the excitement the mad man
began to feel dizzy and a little discombobulated
Regardless, Ollie made time to stop
at the ice cream shop after he masturbated
Then the rascal wished to get raspberry flavor
with sprinkles on a cone
The cashier told him to get out/
Ollie replied, "Bitch, watch your tone!"
He went on to chase shoppers down,
and deliver fierce whacks
with his trusty axe now lodged
in an elderly woman's back
Security utilized a megaphone/
Everyone was instructed to go home
But Ollie was determined to have his fun
before being left alone
Most people would say that yelling back
at the security team is Moot
Ollie stomped a three year old toddler to death inside
a shoe store after trying on combat boots

The cokehead hastily removed them from
his feet because he wished to fell free/ So, please
Bashing in some poor guy's skull will satiate his needs
While skipping merrily through the mall he witnessed
an old man faint
Ollie decided to provide the elderly citizen
with some aid, although
he was far from being a saint
The exhibitionist went up to the second floor/
Despite being nude he still felt hot
He grunted while pushing over the balcony
a hundred pound flower pot
The old man just regained consciousness,
but he still remained on the floor
When it comes to welcoming birthday celebrations,
he won't be having anymore
That enormous potted plant descended
upon the old man as he dread
Before he could move an inch it obliterated his head
The mad man pranced around and whistled
with a feeling of so much glee
The pride that he felt warmed his heart/
How could this possibly be?
Apparently his type of drug addiction
can lead to living a life of ill-will
Ollie's antics soon came to an end
once the police arrived/
They were ordered, shoot to kill

ENJOY YOUR STAY

Welcome to the lavish Patell Medge Resort
The guests are well taken care of by the manager
and his cohorts
Cedric is in charge and provides service with pride
Unbeknownst to the guests,
he and his minions engage in homicide
Last Tuesday a maid named
Melinda went up to the 19th floor
She cleaned a couple of rooms before knocking on Mr.
Willis' door
Old Mr. Willis wasn't alone, as he was accompanied
by his wife
After entering the room,
Melinda picked up a lamp, bludgeoned the woman,
then came the final strike
Everything happened so fast/
Mrs. Willis rolled to the foot of the bed
Melinda promptly pulled out a can of mace,
and went after her husband instead
She sprayed Mr. Willis in the face/
He coughed intensely then he bellowed
The maid picked up a copy of the King James bible
and beat Willis until he mellowed
Melinda reached into her uniform,
and pulled out a knife made of stainless steel
With haste, she slit Mr. Willis' throat while asking,
"How does this feel?"

RECEPTION

The widow tried to crawl away,
but her attempt was futile
Mrs. Willis' head got stomped like grapes in a vineyard/
Her death couldn't be more brutal
In the end it's safe to say that
Mr. and Mrs. Willis did not enjoy their trip
Melinda was very upset when she left
because she didn't receive a tip
A bevy of knocks rattled the entrance of room suite 210
No sooner than Chad Reege answered
the door three men forced their way in
They were all dressed as bellhops/
Trouble is what Chad could foretell
These men are muscle bound/
One cracked his knuckles/ This will not end well
The bellhops were there on the manager's behalf/
Obedient servants in a cult
They didn't hesitate to beat
Chad Reege into a bloody pulp
Later that evening in suite 402
Mr. Sanz was feeling quite nervous
About his business meeting in the morning
but he had to eat/ So, he proceeded to order room service
Half an hour went by/ Sanz was famished/
He wished the food would be delivered in a hurry
The young executive had a taste for Indian cuisine/
His mouth watered for chicken curry
The attendant finally arrived/
Sanz opened the door to the room/

The dinner trolley was pushed inside
A cloche sat on top of the white cloth clad cart,
so everything seemed fine
Mr. Sanz couldn't wait to taste the curry/
He was understandably eager
Without further ado the attendant lifted
the lid to reveal a meat cleaver
The server used it to hack away at
Mr. Sanz and refused to stop
All you could hear were cries
and screams along with the recurrent chop, chop
If you're staying in a room at this resort's hotel,
you are already dead
Don't bother booking a flight home/
Did you hear what I said?
Throughout the day and night cries
for help is what the people here shout
The Grim Reaper is who you'll meet
when the time has come to check out

TAKE HEED IT'S OUR GOLDEN JUBILEE

Geoffrey has been married to Beverly for fifty years
He thought, "Enough is enough,
time to kill you, my dear"
The devoted husband dressed for the occasion/
Paid close attention to detail with care
Being mindful and chivalrous
when pushing his wife down the stairs
Beverly didn't die as a result,
in fact she hardly twitched
Walked away without any injuries/
This outcome left Geoffrey bewitched
The dedicated spouse prepared
for his wife clam chowder,
which happened to contain ground glass
He tried his best not to make his wife's death messy
in an attempt to show some class
Unfortunately, after consuming just one spoonful,
Beverly refused to take another
She said, that the dish wasn't well prepared/
Cooking faux pas, a blunder
Beverly didn't hesitate to criticize her husband/
Can you believe she had the audacity?
When she finally dies from an unnatural
cause it'll hardly be a tragedy
Geoffrey mumbled,

"People will give me their condolences for my loss
Soon the world and I will be rid of you,
you aging albatross
You're putting me in a foul mood/
A closed casket may be
required, which is fantastic
After leaving your gravesite,
I'll be feeling ecstatic
Imagine breathing fresh air for the very first time/
Living life so carefree
Your ashes in an urn are all that I need/
I'll be glad to make you bleed"
One afternoon, his loving wife walked down
the street toward a store where fresh fruit was sold
Beverly nearly avoided being crushed
to death by a collapsing scaffold
The construction workers were very careful
but it wasn't built well from the start
This of course was deliberate/
How else would it fall apart?
There wasn't any negligence on the workers' end/
They were all paid very well
No confessions of felonious acts were made/
No one wished to go to jail
Who was the mastermind behind this devious plot?
Perhaps Beverly's husband is responsible
and he will not stop
until she leaves this life behind/ Buried in a crypt
Today is their anniversary/ Geoffrey bought her a gift

His resentment goes without saying/
When it comes to his anger he's seething
Geoffrey wished to receive the greatest gift of all/
News that his wife is no longer breathing
This marriage has been a farce/ Indubitably a disgrace
The man couldn't bear to wake up
one more morning and see Beverly's face
Geoffrey said, "Apparently, I'll never have a chance
to live life to the fullest,
but I certainly can't live with you
This hell on Earth must come to an end/
There's something that I must do
Here is a present for you on our special day/
The answer to all of our problems are hidden within"
Beverly joyously unwrapped the gift
which was a grenade/
Geoffrey immediately pulled the pin
His wife seemed to be flabbergasted
before she howled and screamed
Finally Geoffrey saw a glimmer of hope,
as they were both blown to smithereens

FAST FOOD FATALITY

Hi, welcome to McGobble/ May I take your order?
No, I'm here to see Linda/ I have something for her
She knows why I have a grievance/
Wait a second, that's you
You don't seem to recognize me/
Just came from the drive-thru
I paid for a BLT sandwich
and chicken tenders with honey
The bag only contained half-eaten garlic bread/
Did you really think that shit was funny?
Please don't bother answering/ It's a rhetorical question
What a wonder/ The female mind/
Should I blame the estrogen?
Is that what made you think you can get away with this?
Feel free to welcome my grand return/
Now I'm really pissed
You are quite the comedian/ It's our destiny to meet
Fortunately, I had something
in my car laid out on the backseat
The blade was sharpened only recently/
It's the perfect tool
for dishing out some justice/
Out of me you made a fool
In this life ambition is required to get ahead,
and I'll gladly take your head
Promote your decapitated corpse to "an extra"
on The Walking Dead

You turn away as if you're bored
What do you think the machete is for?
It's about to become extremely exciting here in a minute
I'm telling you the truth/ Don't be such a cynic
I can see that you're feeling extraordinarily dismayed
With a swing of my blade
I'll hack all of your problems away
Why are you so quiet now?/
You don't have anything to say?
I promise that you won't have to worry
about living another day
Tell your customers to stop screaming/
Sir, please calm down
There's a sure fire, not so subtle way,
to rearrange that frown
Have a seat, Mister/ You don't want to miss
the rest of the show
Before I give you a permanent smile
in the form of a glasgow
Ah, back to Linda/
You made your co-workers laugh, I'm glad
But if you mistakenly assumed
you will reach age thirty that's too bad
Don't you dare start crying/
I'm not falling for your crocodile tears
If you were ever afraid of growing old
I'll be erasing all of your fears
Why on earth are you quivering?/
There isn't any reason for you to be anxious

I strongly advise you to cut that shit before
I lose my patience
Now it's too late/
Perhaps with that little stunt you pulled your
co-workers gave you praise
With this decapitation your head hits the floor,
and you still don't get a raise
What a mess to clean up/
Regarding your inevitable death was
there ever any doubt?
There isn't any overtime for bleeding
all over the place and you forgot to clock out

IT'S KID OR BE KILLED

Hey mommy, I'm going outside to play
Always walking a rocky narrow path but I'll never sway
Insistent on remaining diligent all throughout the day
How many of the kids that I know will pass away?
A high quantity is preferred/
Anything less isn't suitable
If things go my way the count may become innumerable
Most of the adults refer to me as being precocious
A ten year old scientific prodigy that
can easily create explosives
I made one then placed it next door
on the side of the garage
Billy lives there and I hate him,
but I bid him bon voyage
It brings tears to my eyes knowing
that I brought forth Billy's cessation
When the explosive went off
I couldn't stop applauding/
Gave myself a standing ovation
This morning mom and dad wanted me
to eat breakfast, so I finished all of my oatmeal
Left the house soon after to go find Luis/
His impending death will give me a thrill
However, before I left the table my brother
Frankie was there/ He's six
He has a tendency to be a tattle tale/
That self righteous little prick

Suddenly both of my parents left the kitchen/
This was my golden opportunity
Then my little brother had to go use the bathroom/
I must hurry so no one will see
We had a lot of laughs, baby bro/
Mommy thinks from Heaven you were sent
After you finish your cereal,
you'll be on your way to Hell/
I mixed in some laundry detergent
Frankie has always been a goody two shoes/
He always does as he's told
When my brother returned he clumsily swung his arm,
accidentally knocking over the bowl
This mishap occurred before Frankie could eat,
which of course made my blood boil
His careless act is all it takes
for my master plan to be foiled
After leaving the house I found
Luis hanging out down the street
A fifth grade bully that's rather rotund
and cannot wait to eat
He decided the other day at recess
that he wanted to play with my toy truck
But then he refused to give it back/ Dude, what the fuck?
That fat boy smiled when he saw me/
He should really consider eating a salad
I smiled as well while holding behind
my back an iron mallet
Luis held some other kid's stolen toy

which was soon dropped after he stumbled
Because I beat him mercilessly/
Later his parents discovered him bloodied and pummeled
I want to grow up to be the very best
at this without a shadow of a doubt
That afternoon, Leo and I played
Cowboys and Indians/ I couldn't wait to take his scalp
This tough ol' cowboy ran behind a tree,
hiding in the shade
Unbeknownst to him I had my trusty tomahawk/
He'll be sure to taste my blade
Suddenly Leo stuck his head out from
behind the tree/ This game is loads of fun
The cowboy thought he had the drop on me
and pulled out his toy guns
Leo drew his weapons while extremely eager
to take aim with them
I snuck up from behind,
and embedded the tomahawk into his cranium
Well, I'm afraid it's getting late,
and I don't want Mom and Dad to get peeved
There isn't enough time to give you a proper burial,
so I'll just cover you up with these leaves
Some would say, I had my way/
At least I made that bully pay
There are other kids in my neighborhood
and tomorrow's another day

SADISTIC THERAPY SESSION

Good morning Dr. Lansing, isn't it a lovely day?
Let me tell you about all the good people that I slayed
The other night I crept through
a neighborhood located in Beverly Hills
I'm so damn poor, people there should know exactly how I feel
Truth be told,
I'm upper middle class but my victims weren't aware
of the deal Couldn't tell if it was a dream/
It all seemed so surreal
I performed a home invasion/
Shot and killed a man and his wife
Their two children ran away sobbing/ Hey, that's life
On Wednesday I had a date
Mary showed up late at my place but she looked great
Gorgeous gal that makes you say, wow
Using only your inner monologue/
It shouldn't be said out loud
This date happened to be our third/
I'll be blunt, she didn't survive
Mary wished to stay overnight/
What else could I do but skin her alive?
That lovely lady forced me to strap her down/She
struggled and would not behave
Then I presented Mary with a straight razor to give her
a very close shave I assure you that it was of excellent quality/
Superior to the rest

The blade wasn't intended for trimming hair
but best used for removing flesh
Mary begged me to let her go, and she insisted
that I'm not sane
If that were true would I have kept her conscious
in order to feel the excruciating pain?
I proceeded in peeling her skin gingerly
as if she were an avocado
Before dying, Mary endured the most agonizing torment
most deserving of praise, bravo
Acts like these grant me self gratification/
This is my true incentive
Plus, I also did it for Mary, herself because
I'm extremely caring and attentive
Yesterday I was seduced by Nadine,
then she brought me back to her home
What in the world came over me?/
Must've been the pheromones
This sultry cat had me in her shack/
Nadine was into rough sex and wanted a few slaps
But I had a much better idea that involved
the utilization of a bear trap
After all, this is a rural area
which explains why she had the trap in the first place
Wild life lurked around every corner/
She bought it just in case
Instantaneously a kinky idea entered my mind/
It kept me buzzing like a bee
I stripped Nadine naked,

covered her with honey, then tied her to a tree
This is the most unusual circumstance
because it didn't require me to force
my victim to come outside in the nude
and let nature take its course
Before long I heard a growl/ On my face a grin
A grizzly bear appeared that had a taste
for honey glazed women
Nadine shrieked at the top of her lungs/
That scream chilled me to the bone
I assured Nadine that everything will work out
for the best/ "I'll watch the outcome from your home"
With haste, I ran inside then looked through
the window/ What happened next... oh, Jesus
I watched in delight as the that 800 pound
grizzly tore Nadine to pieces
Well, I know that our time is almost up/Everything I said
is confidential
I'm a little apprehensive/ I believe you'll tell just because
I'm a little mental
There's only one way to live this life/
I'll do whatever I please
Now that I have my hands around your throat, do you
mind if I squeeze?
Dr. Lansing even though you're dead I'm glad that we were
able to start this
Therapy is something that actually works, causing me to
achieve a catharsis

GORY GOURMET

The meat for my latest dish has been braised
It is hell that I will raise
Do you like my new dress?/ I'm a little distressed
Benjamin's now a corpse/ Of course he's a bloody mess
I did remove all of his entrails/ That I must confess
Sent this man to heaven/ Where's my halo?/ God bless
They refer to me as a deviant/ Whatever I desire I'll get
Ate some severed testicles/
Topped them off with a little orange sherbet
This might sound a little crazy,
although I want you to follow
me in eating a spleen steamed, eyeballs and gelato
Thinly sliced butt cheeks/ Give them a pinch
of salt/ Not my fault Katie hasn't been seen since
She was quickly abducted after asking me for a ride
Once Katie got inside of my car
it's the equivalent to suicide
Always wanted to be the best/ I'm continuing to strive
Making meals out of my victims/
That deserves a high five
Beth's head has been broiled/
The rest of her carcass is in the tub
Her desire was to take a bubble bath/
Body submerged in soap suds
My severed human breasts are the best served
with simmering hot brocolii
An agonizing death is what you'll experience

if you dare to engage in mocking me
Have a pair of filet of feet chopped fresh today
They came from a repugnant cab driver/
I had to make him pay
Carved out a huge portion of his back/
Prepared it as if it were a brisket
Cooked it slowly/ So savory/
One taste and you'll want to finish it
Never waste an ounce of quality meat/
Cut it down to the bone
If you have some "cabbie" left over you're allowed
to take a doggy bag home
My latest victim was given a knife blade swiftly
to the navel
Soon enough he ceased struggling
because he was no longer able
This particular murder occurred
in broad daylight/ Frankly, I took quite a risk
Goop was dripping from his stomach/
It was used to make lobster bisque
Anyone that has tasted my cooking always has my back
especially if they've eaten
my succulent seared scrotum sac
It's best to stay out of my kitchen/
Everyone here should know
You don't want to be within my presence
while I'm slaving over a hot stove

AN OBESE THANKSGVING

Craig Wellterz is a big boy,
although he doesn't play with toys
Thirty-eight years old,
cramming food down is his pride and joy
Weighing almost 400 pounds/ Regardless, he gets around
The expanding matter/ He's getting fatter/
Can you hear that sound?
Today is Thanksgiving/
In the home where Craig is living
There are a multitude of visitors/
Craig won't be forgiving
anyone that prevents him from stuffing his face
Most of these relatives don't reside here,
so they must learn their place
Until all of the food is gone, Craig will not be done
He'll be systematically picking off relatives one by one
There stood Uncle Abel he knew Craig
since he was in the cradle
Less attendance is required at the dining room table
Craig caught Abel outside of the bathroom/
It has a sink with a leaky faucet
He hit Abel on the head with a pipe wrench
then dragged him into his bedroom closet
Uncle Abel is dead as a doornail /
How does this make Craig feel?
Famine is upon him/
Cannot wait to indulge in tonight's grand meal

The rotund man felt dehydrated/
Doesn't drink water but I'll mention
Craig has a bottle of soda, he's sipping,
actually gulping on his way to the kitchen
He said, "None of these fools should
disturb my mother and auntie/
We want to avoid any cooking blunders
I must find something in the meantime to satiate my hunger"
While frothing at the mouth,
Craig stood there desiring to consume
Mama said, "Have some fruit"/
Her son replied, "Bitch, are you
serious? This isn't a cartoon"
After leaving the kitchen with the intention
of dispatching more relatives
Craig climbed the stairs and reached
the second floor which is without a doubt, imperative
He knocked on the door of a bedroom
and entered where his grandparents stay
Craig's grandfather stood in grandiose,
and refused to get out of his way
The elder told Craig to lose weight,
but this isn't a day that he can afford
for tempers to flare/ Craig strangled
his grandfather with his own catheter cord
His death really is for the best/ An ornery old man who
talked about Craig getting fatter
Grandma was present and became irate/ She forced Craig
to slap her

Then he led his grandmother to an open window,
and forced her head down on the sill
Craig promptly took away her oxygen tank
because she wouldn't keep still
Extensive counts of over-exertion
caused the woman's hyperventilation
The window was forced shut
with all of Craig's might, resulting in
his grandmother's decapitation
Conduct from the old lady wasn't acceptable,
and the grandfather behaved like a douche
The severed head of Craig's grandmother
fell like a soccerball into a bush
Craig rummaged through his grandfather's
belongings, and found a loaded luger,
then descended down the stairs
Most of his relatives were in the living room
watching a football game/
The trigger of that gun was pulled, I do declare
The murder of Craig's father,
two brothers, and cousins were all mercilessly done
It's unfortunate that they died prior
to the conclusion of the game/
Now they'll never know who won
The table was set and the food has been served
At gunpoint Craig's mother and aunt
wouldn't dare double-cross him/
They didn't have the nerve
They were truly petrified

and didn't know what to do
Whenever Craig gets this riled up
it's like feeding time at the zoo
Craig sat down and ate/ Then he screamed,
"The pumpkin pie is gone!/ God, tell me why?!"
The aunt replied, "Your brothers ate it all"/
Craig said, "That's not true, you lie"
His aunt was ordered to have a seat,
then Craig shot her in the head
The gluttonous man continued
to eat as the dead woman sat there and bled
Food was devoured at the speed of light/
Craig's mother continued to serve dinner and avoid harm
Her voracious son cleared off plate after plate/
This is a legitimate reason for alarm
A mouth full of turkey and potato salad/
Craig began to clutch his chest
He swallowed it all despite choking,
determined to eat the rest
Suddenly, Craig fell face first
into his plate piled high with dressing
His mother gave a sigh of relief/
The time had come for eternal resting
Compassion is something that
this glutton had always lacked
He was bloated then died after suffering
a festive heart attack

BRUTALITY AT ITS FINEST

What is that we do while enjoying our little dance?
Visit you while you're sleeping
with a jar of flesh eating ants
Watching with anticipation/ Whistling while they work
They're eating so much of you/
It makes me want to burp
Can't believe that this worked/
The insects were persistently doing their jobs
Rapidly ravaged you like you're corn on the cob
Lord forgive me not/ I'll just repeat the process
Others will do my bidding/ Get me another hostage
No way, I will not barter/ There isn't anything to trade
Recently kidnapped a woman/ Damn it, I lost my blade
There's nothing to fear/ Don't you cry, my dear
Came back from the toolshed
with a pair of pruning shears
The task at hand will be completed/
Diligently working one on one
Treating you like an unkempt garden/
This'll be so much fun
Cutting off all of your fingers/
Snipping away your ears
Your cries of misery nearly brought me to tears
Time to use a garden hoe/ That's the way to go
Forget all about those feet/ Say good bye to your toes
Feels good to put your hands in the soil,
providing some landscaping

Don't bother screaming for help/
You will not be escaping
Full display of hatred in your eyes/
Please don't be angry with me
If you were to leave that'll be a catastrophe
I've already had my fun with you/
Without feet you won't get far
Throw you into my cellar/ You'll probably starve
On to my next victim/
Picked up a hitchhiker during a rainstorm
Covered her mouth with a handkerchief
drenched in chloroform
Once my lady regained consciousness
she did not open her eyes
I have already taken them/
What a splendid surprise
This woman became hysterical/
Give it a little time
Must be difficult to adjust
when you first discover that you're blind
On top of the mantle your eyeballs sit so you can
always see that you're an absolute dream
and what you mean to me
Proposition of marriage is on my mind,
but I must take your liver
Yeah, I think that I'll kill you instead/
Dump your body in the river
Jesus is our savior/ To him we all must pray
Then I'll be back out on the road searching for more prey

THE RIGHT TO BEAR HARM

Regarding the laws of the constitution,
my favorite is the second amendment
The founding fathers found a lust for blood/
I for one share this sentiment
The brilliance of these men do not escape me/
It's not out of place
To think they were aware of plausible altercations,
and the need to blow off someone's face
Personally, a life of peace and leisure is what
I actively pursue
I'm still awake having a little nightcap/
It's currently ten after two
A little welcoming committee
just showed up at my backdoor
Don't you know it's the middle of the night?/
What the hell are they here for?
Four would-be assailants are breaking and entering
Society has failed them/ At a younger age,
should've had some mentoring
Soon they will have many regrets similar
to a bad marriage
We're all in this together now,
but I'll make sure they eventually perish
Silly me, did I forget to mention my fondness of guns?
Copious amounts of artillery fully stocked/

I'm bound to have some fun
Time to do my country proud/
Salute the American flag
Didn't hesitate to accumulate ammunition
then placed it inside of a bag
Each man separated before running
any kind of reconnaissance
Creeping around in the dark doesn't make any sense
I found one of those bastards,
and gave him a twenty-one gun salute to his belly
Believe me when I say,
the AR-15 has never ever failed me
Another thief I shot in the kidneys/
No where near the spine/
Therefore, an avoidance of paralysis
I said, "Regrettably I'll give you my analysis/
You're going to require dialysis."
Will you stop squirming and squealing
on my kitchen floor?
Soaking wet, sweating profusely
from each and every pore
This is what happens
when you enter someone's home and it isn't permissible
Don't expect me to be courteous
or the least bit hospitable
Without notice I pulled a knife,
persistently stabbing my pin cushion friend
Sorry to say, if I had the chance I'd do it all over again
Any attempt to track me in the dark is not at all wise

One of the men became startled when I yelled,
"Surprise!"
Gun in hand, I pulled the trigger/
That man lost his mind, literally
My carpet is now covered with brain matter
and a quart of his pee
During the hunt I eventually found the final degenerate
So much fear in his eyes,
giving the stare of solemn regret
I said, "Your friends were extracted
virtually without any fight
There's a sense of your feelings of perilous plight
All of you are the equivalent of rodents
which are unwanted pests
At least you won't have to seek medical treatment/
I'll gladly put you to rest"
The trigger was pulled vehemently
with an abundance of zeal and zest
A 44 magnum was utilized to blow open his chest
Then I said, "In case you weren't aware
I didn't do it for glory, and
I'm certainly not to blame
If it's any consolation we'll all be on the six o'clock
news for 15 minutes of fame"

ONCE A CHEATER, ALWAYS A BLEEDER

My name is Peggy Sue/ Failed relationships are my forte
They never end well which is a fairly simple
point to relay
What should be duly noted here are the reasons why/
All integral circumstances
The men involved were never seen again/
They don't receive any second chances
Back in high school I was made a fool
Lost my virginity to my boyfriend but it wasn't cool
Soon afterward I was dumped by the inconsiderate slob
Quarterback on the football team/
Go long, his name was Rob
He attempted to drive me home/
We were sitting at a traffic stop
When I stabbed him vivaciously
with a knife that was well crafted in metal shop
Apparently my study partner is dead/
He's never returning to class
Had a math test the next morning/
My concern was that I wouldn't pass
Years later, my boyfriend cheated on me/
A drug dealer named Seth
Caught in a meth lab explosion,
resulting in an instant death
This is the perfect opportunity to let loose,

dance, cut a rug
Let this be a lesson, kids/ Always say no to drugs
If there is something I can never understand
It's infidelity and my inability to keep a man
Soon enough I had a gentleman caller/
His name was Rufus
Quite cunning and just as conniving,
but I'm never clueless
One day I came home and discovered a lady
with Rufus in bed, nothing to it
I struck a match after dousing
both parties with lighter fluid
The couple were laid to rest,
so the degenerates remained in bed
Both burnt to a crisp with smoke emanating
from their heads
This predicament saddened me even though
Rufus loved to cheat
The bedroom furniture will be sorely missed
and those were expensive sheets
Eventually I found the man of my dreams/
That's why we have a marriage
Not much longer, there'll be a dissolution/
He's been prophesized to perish
It's a tale of the seven year itch,
but we've only been together for three
Benny has already committed numerous acts of adultery
Finally I ascertained his floozy's location/
She was staying at a hotel

Under inexplicable circumstances,
from the eleventh floor she fell
to her death on Dundee Road/
Isn't that just dandy?
She wasn't sweet/ Life for her went sour/
Ironically her name was Candi
My husband is a successful executive,
quickly climbing the corporate ladder
He hired Lilly, a gorgeous 23-year-old secretary,
claiming that age doesn't matter
It didn't take long for them to start sleeping together/
One night when she was home alone
I broke into Lilly's house, stripped her naked,
and remembered to smash her cell phone
Tied her up utilizing extension cords/
It seems that Benny will miss
this reality/ Get a grip with a pair of pliers/
Yes, I mean her clitoris
It didn't take too long, I twisted and turned,
eventually pried it off with pride
To see Lilly incapacitated,
now passed out from pain it makes me feel warm inside
Keeping her gagged the entire time
was a wise decision, because
she struggled to scream and shout
My wish was to take a tour of Lilly's lovely home
but she bled to death/
Guess I'll show myself out
Benny's desire is to carry on

with his infinite discretions
I've finally decided to leave him behind
but not before my confession
Regarding my husband's latest sexual escapade
there's a price he already paid
I personally provided the woman/
Full disclosure, she has full blown AIDS

HIPPOCRATIC OATH DENIED

Hello, I'm Dr. Vicento, Plastic Surgeon/
How are you today?
Sorry to say, that I'm here ill-prepared for the day
A hangover can cause me to be late to the scene
but I'll always be adamant about showing up
because I want the green
The gold, the jewels, let's operate on these fools
Surgery in a hurry with unsterilized medical tools
Follow protocol and pay the money upfront/
There are no exceptions
Thoughts of you getting a surgical infection
can cause me an erection
Currently I'm not plastered still it's pitiful and flaccid
Patients checking my credentials is a dirty little habit
to break like your nose/ Doesn't matter
if you're scheduled for rhinoplasty
If something goes wrong your blood pressure
will drop faster than gravity
I had an extremely wealthy patient this week/
Has pizzazz and he's a baller
We scheduled him for a penis enlargement,
so I made it smaller
Operations are conducted by following
a strict moral code
More money means that

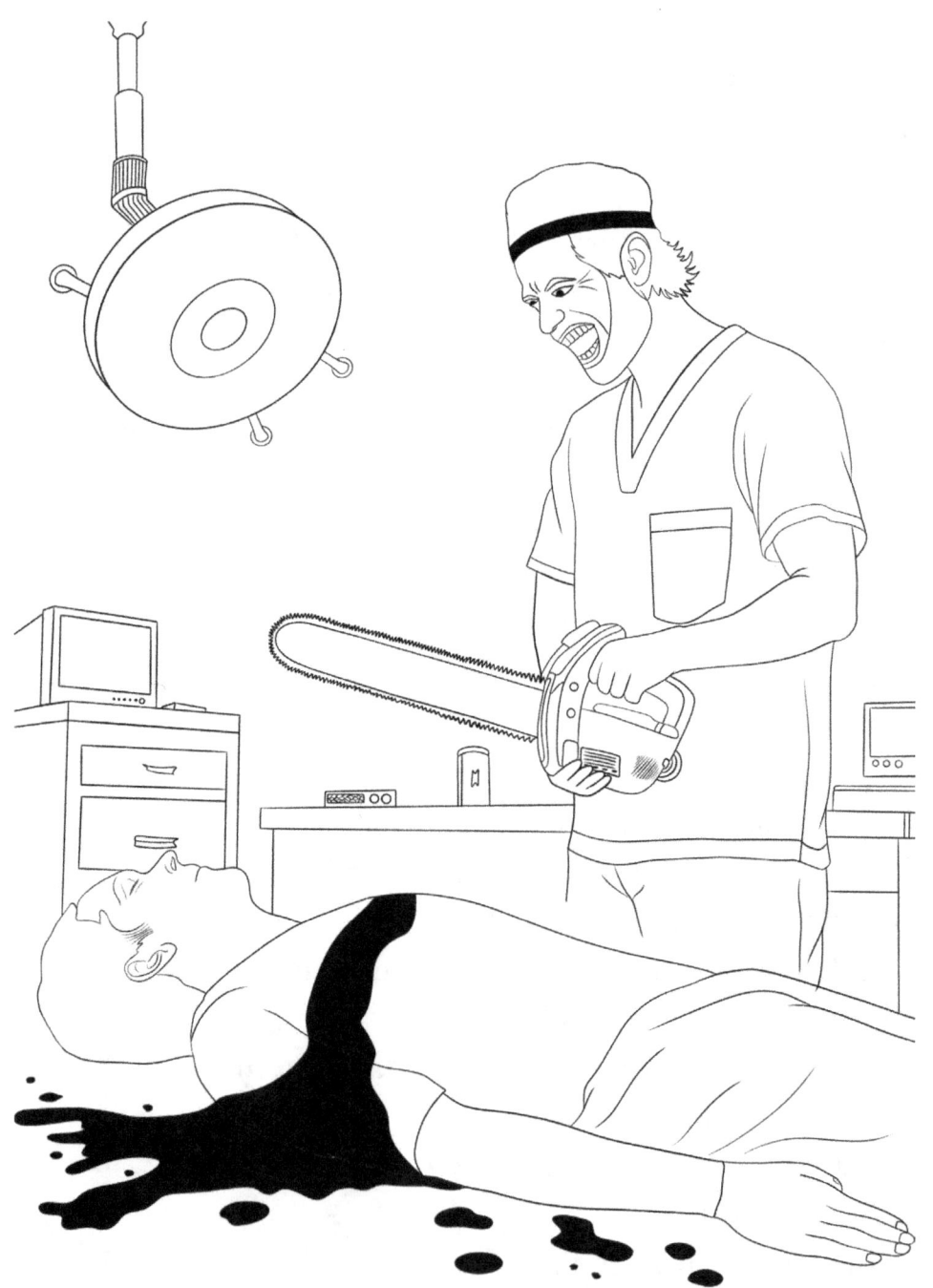

I can add a west wing to my humble abode
A woman was scheduled for breast augmentation/
There might've been a slight complication
As a joke I deliberately made her breasts asymmetrical/
With a lack of oxygen she required resuscitation
We were unsuccessful at reviving the patient then
I received a low blow
Her family had the gall to sue me for liability/
I didn't enjoy that part of the show
Another female patient desired breast implants/
We refused to use silicone
Her chest is now filled with grape jelly/
She should've left them alone
I'm often asked, "Why do you like to play
God with people's lives?"
These patients of mine should feel grateful
just to make it out alive
Statistically, that's not always the case
Sometimes I get distracted with social media
and make a mistake
Time for the procedure/
Your chance of survival is at fifteen percent
Choosing me as your plastic surgeon
is a decision that makes very little sense
Best to have a little wine/ It improves my competency
Then I'm slightly less likely
to inadvertently sever an artery
The anesthesiologist took the day off,
so I'll perform the procedure

while you're still awake
It's most probable that you'll pass out
from the pain, hopefully for your sake
My medical team is inexperienced/
If they screw up try to be forgiving
But don't burden yourself with those fine details/
You won't be returning to the land of the living
When you get to Heaven and meet Saint Peter tell him
I said, hello, when you greet him
Chest compressions didn't work/ Patient flatlined/
Time of death is 3:18 pm

TRUTH OR DIE

Good times and memories from the days
at my alma mater
Remembering is hardly difficult
when you bear witness to a slaughter
I'll be forthcoming and admit that I facilitated the event
That led to the deaths of multiple college students
and their afterlife descent
It involved an innocent co-ed gathering
at the Gentro Fraternity
I merely suggested that we play a game/
Enjoyment was practically a certainty
Several titles were mentioned/ I said,
"They're all dull"/ Then
someone asked me, "Why?"
I replied, "Let's play something with a modified twist/
How about Truth Or Die?"
Most of the participants were inebriated,
holding liquor filled plastic cups
For anyone disconnected from reality
this will sober them right up
Everyone must abide by the rules of the game
no matter how intense this gets or offensive
Any deviation from set directives
may result in dire consequences
All participants must follow through
with the choices they make/
That's not asking for a lot

In my hand I hold a semi-automatic
pistol for those that want to get shot
Sarah was asked, Truth or dare?/
She chose dare, and was eager to compete/ I told ya
That was prior to instructions that were given to drink a
quarter of this bottle of ammonia
I wasn't currently in the best of moods,
so I didn't wish to scold
this young lady for not playing along,
but she eventually did as she was told
A beverage of this sort doesn't tend to go down smoothly
If there was any chance Sarah enjoyed her drink,
without a doubt you could've fooled me
Sarah began to curse and violently convulse/
Didn't seem that anyone could stop this
Far from being a pleasant feeling, I'm sure/
The chemical severely burned her esophagus
Before dropping dead my only hope is that
Sarah had learned a lesson
Damned if I knew what it was supposed to be/
On to the next contestant
Martin was asked the question and chose truth/
He genuinely thought this choice would save him
I asked Martin if he ever engaged in any infidelity/
No where to run to or safe haven
He answered, yes, within his girlfriend's presence/
Soon Martin will see the light
Before asking the question I was considerate enough to
hand Penelope a butcher knife

In a pit of rage, Penelope stabbed her boyfriend so fast it made me dizzy
She did it thirty-one more times just for laughs/
You're in a lot of trouble now, Missy
There's a catharsis from what she did/
Penelope was devoid of remorse
Without skipping a beat, she leaned over in her seat to spit on her boyfriend's corpse
Then I asked Wanda, "Truth or dare?"/
She replied, "Dare," for a kick
She was instructed to sodomize her good friend Ted with the end of a broomstick
Teddy wouldn't allow this to happen/
What an intriguing prick
Since he refused to participate, I chose to end him quick
I pulled the trigger of my colt 45/
A bullet passed through Ted's lung
Almost everybody screamed when he hit the floor/
What, aren't you having any fun?
Then I decided to play Duck, Duck, Goose,
but it was more like Duck, Duck, Dead
If you were to become the chosen one,
you'll quickly receive a bullet to the head
Apparently, Russell couldn't take it anymore/
He was nearly ready to flee
I picked up a sledge hammer contiguous to me,
and used it smash in both of his knees
Such a sad state of affairs/
Crawling across the floor still attempting to leave

Placed my foot on his neck, and continued
to do so until he could no longer breathe
No one seemed to be enjoying themselves/
Eventually I bid all of my classmates adieu
Earlier, I set C-4 in a corner,
made sure to be far away when it blew
Now I spend my days inside a happy home,
devoid of an penitence
All of that happened nearly nine years ago/
Sure feels good to Reminisce

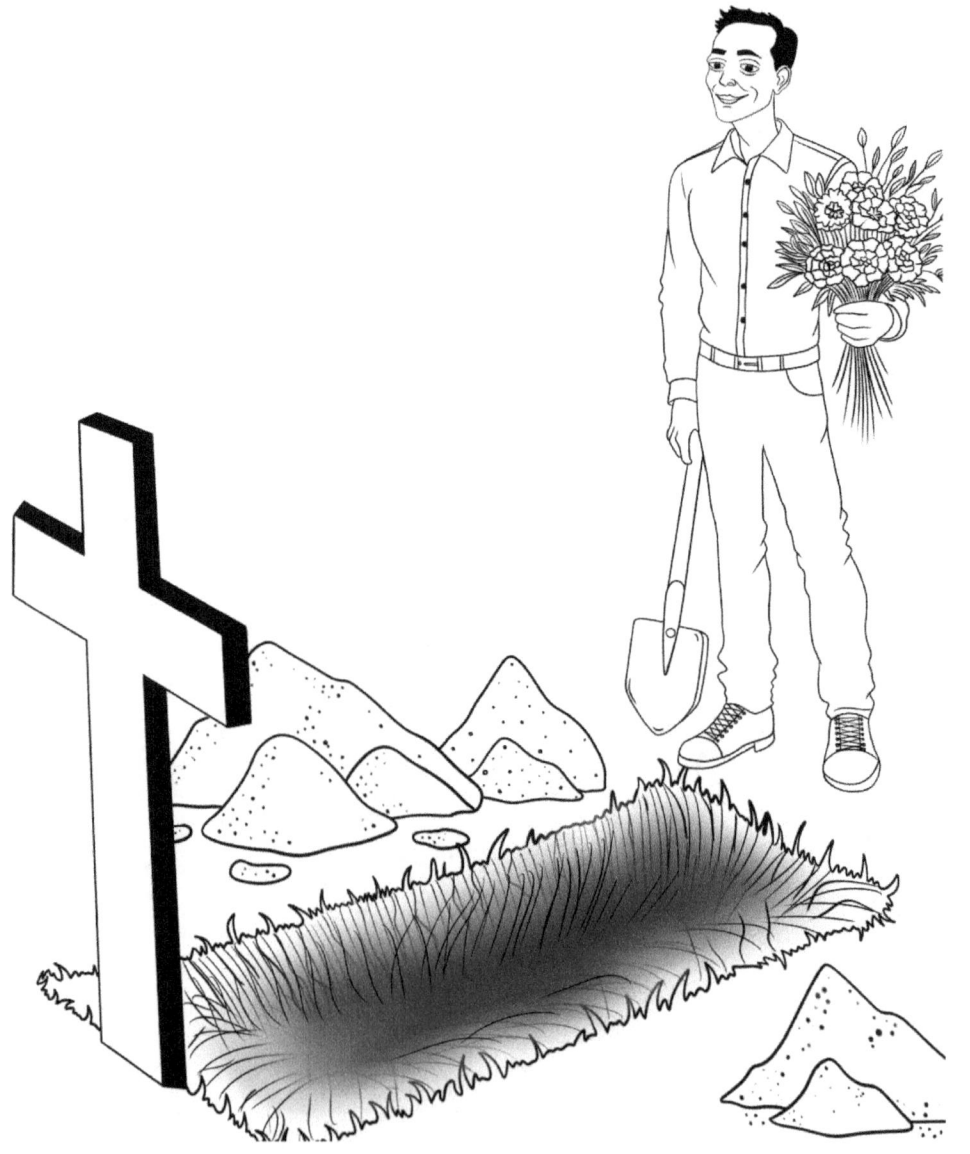

AN ENTANGLEMENT WITH THE DEAD

Say hello to Jolene/ Barney dug her up from the grave
Brought her home with the intention
of turning her into a sex slave
Altruism should be taken into consideration/
Barney merely wished to save this woman from rotting
without a purpose, and the body that he craved
However, a gentleman always keeps his composure
and treats a lady right
They'll be plenty of time for hanky panky
later in the night
Bound by love, Benny will do his best to preserve
the cadaver/ He's not stupid
Jolene was buried over a week ago,
and in dire need of more embalming fluid
It's sad to say, that ship has sailed/
Living in denial will affect Barney's decision
To carry on/ Clearly the corpse has already
begun its decomposition
Time had been taken to reapply the cadaver's make up/
Barney chose to utilize care and patience
A putrid stench filled the room/
Jolene was sprayed with her favorite perfume fragrance
Concerns were being raised in Barney's mind
that his lady was becoming combative
Because she didn't like the dress

that Barney chose for her/
Even cadavers can look attractive
An extensive argument ensued,
but eventually Barney got his way
He said, "You should learn to appreciate everything \
I do for you/ That's all I have to say"
Of course, the woman didn't say anything
at all because she's already dead
A harsh reality Barney was incapable
of getting into his head
Or maybe he did and in all honesty preferred it that way
There is a certain desirability in rigor mortis
and the appearance of decay
Perhaps this was meant to be/
During Jolene's life, Barney had only seen her once
She was speaking with her unruly friends,
a bunch of loud mouth gibbering cunts
Everybody in the neighborhood heard
about Jolene's untimely passing
A minister stated at the funeral
she will go on with Jesus Christ, life everlasting
Someone driving under the influence,
struck the young pedestrian/
Her parents were saddened but pissed
Witnessing Jolene on the slab is an experience,
Barney didn't want to miss
Fast forward to the present/ A lady lost her life/
Lights in the room became slightly dimmer
Being such a romantic at heart,

Barney prepared a candlelight dinner
The sight of this rotting corpse
with flies buzzing about, placed Barney into a trance
Then he got up and walked over to it and asked,
"My lady, may I have this dance?"
Barney was delirious with delight/
What else could he wish for?
Music played as he held up Jolene's corpse
and dragged it across the floor
Finally once the dance had ended,
Jolene was carried off to the bedroom
Some would say, this is morally defunct/
She should be resting in a tomb
Barney couldn't stand the odor/
Jolene was sprayed with a fresh body mist
Then the young man leaned toward the corpse,
and gave it a passionate kiss
Both parties were laid out on the bed/
Barney disrobed then helped Jolene
This was subsequent to asking permission first,
because he did not wish to demean
His lady love from Heaven above/
Actually it was the ground below
Wearing nothing but high heels/
The corpse had lost weight and it really shows
If Jolene is not careful she'll become skin and bones
Ha, ha, the young man is ecstatic
to have her inside of his home
In fact, Barney wished to please his lady/

He was compelled to go down south
After performing cunnilingus,
Barney had to pick maggots out of his mouth
More foreplay ensued then on to the main event
Forty-five minutes passed
and the man was completely spent
Some people were convinced that
Barney could never have her
Jolene made a damn fine looking cadaver
Back when the young woman
was still alive she had the potential to become an actress
Regardless, the corpse was kicked out of bed/
Barney didn't like to cuddle,
and he had to shake the worms off of his mattress
It's a necessity to discard the body/
Barney thought, "Can't allow anyone to see us"
Fun and games are over now/
Purge fluid is still dripping from his penis
Most certainly this was a special moment in time/
No need for opposing personalities to clash
Barney thanked Jolene for a lovely evening,
then put her out on the curb with the rest of the trash

SUMMER CAMP PRISON

Hi Mom and Dad, Sure do hope that you get this letter
I'm twenty-four years old and in prison/Can life possi-
bly get any better?
Wish I could say,
I'm having a swell time while doing time
Made a wise decision to pay Bruno for protection,
so I'm doing fine
Yesterday at lunch a man approached Ronaldo/
He demanded to be given his fruit cup
Then another sneaky guy with a shank came
from behind and cut Ronaldo up
Make no mistake, this is a sad outcome/
Ronaldo was my best friend
Life is full of ups and downs, mostly downs,
when you're staying at the state pen
Today in arts and crafts we made macaroni necklaces/
Wayne gave one to his bitch
That's what Darren now Denise had become after
it was discovered that he's actually a snitch
One rule of conduct that must always be observed, never
be a tattle tale
Or life will become much more difficult to bear in this
living hell
Everyday I do pushups in my cell/
It's the safest way to workout in my opinion
In the yard, Jackson used a fifty pound
dumbbell against another inmate,

easily caved his skull in
Torrance made a lot of enemies during his stay/
Only had four months to go
He tried his best to avoid conflict, but trouble will always follow
him everywhere/During a collect call with his wife he seemed very excited while on the phone
This inmate officially became a short timer,
couldn't wait to get himself home
Finally, only six days to go/ God is such a tease
Someone slit Torrance's throat in his sleep/
That's one way to be granted early release
Nevin is known for his lack of good manners/
Typically in a state that seems irate
He doesn't allow his cellmate to pee standing up/
Stephen must be seated while he urinates
If you're willing to kill on the behalf of gangs
you'll be paid a handsome amount
They'll deposit a couple of grand
into your commissary account
My participation was imminent/
Delivering pain and a world of hurt
Had to happen, couldn't be helped/
I wanted to buy this cool new shirt
Luckily, it's in my size and style
with an awesome design
My cellmate just finished making a brand
new batch of toilet wine
This is not proper timing for a celebratory drink/

I've been feeling a little tense
Since learning that the guy who paid me is a rat/
He's turning state evidence
If this goes to trial and I'm found guilty,
I'll be doing life, so I can't lose
Just because I committed murder
for this shirt and a nice pair of shoes
At the end of the trial I was found guilty,
then transferred to a cell where I stay alone
It's located on death row,
which has become my new home
So, mom and dad, it's been a lot of laughs
I murdered and maimed on a prison gang's behalf
This truly is a fine state institution
Hopefully you'll come and visit me
on the day of my execution
My appeals have run out/ You may sooner or later
grab your popcorn and watch me gasp
for air in the gas chamber
Well, this is a long letter/
I don't wish to be a bore
I'm signing off now, Truly yours, Gary

NEVER BREAK
A BAD HABIT

Have to have the cash/ Willing to sell my ass
I'm a volatile drug addict/ My dealer and I will clash
Goddamn squirrels, lowly critters/Yes, I have the jitters
Can't crack the combination to this safe,
but I'm not a quitter
Diseases, fully infected/ My strive flawlessly infectious
I'll do anything to support my habit/
Exhibiting behavior that's deemed reckless
Life is the juice that I imbibe/
It's a miracle that I'm still alive
Never the simplest hint of sobriety, struggling to survive
Cease being an incorrigible catalyst/
A deceitful little prick
This is causing me to become truculent/
Need to get my fix
You know very well what I paid for/
Your home must be explored
Holding out on me isn't a wise decision/
I'm clearly desperate for more
Where do you hide your stash?/
Feel free to relinquish the drugs
I'll break open every wall in your house,
lift up and look under every rug
Are you feeling obligated to pay the price?/ It wasn't
very nice

that you attempted to rip me off/ A pound of coke
will suffice
My hatred might be slightly out of place
Really can't stand the sight of your face
I already killed your lovely wife/
Don't care if I leave a trace
of evidence in this residence/
Soon you'll also be erased
from existence/ For instance,
I brought along this chain saw
Ask me if I care that murder one is against the law
If I may say so, this happened to be a sound investment
What's the matter,
there isn't any intention for you to contest it?
Weaselly, whining goat, death is looming just accept it
Sorry, but your upper body and legs will no longer be
connected
So, you decided to give me the powder, because I wield
the power
of the chainsaw/ Your frequent squirming causes me
to cringe, you coward
Large quantities of candy/ Watch how it goes
With my disappearing trick/ Abracadabra/
All up my nose
Now was that so hard?/ I'll rev up the chainsaw
Should've given it to me in the first place/
You'll be shredded like coleslaw
Don't mean to be mean, but I love to hear you scream
Trash bags filled with your body parts

thrown into a stream
Wash away your worries/
The future is becoming blurry
Can you see we're running out of time?/
I'm in a bit of a hurry
I'm swinging this chainsaw with admiration/
Don't feel as though you're being attacked
Did you even stop to notice
that your left arm is no longer attached?
I almost gave up hope,
then you eventually gave me my coke
You honestly thought you could get away with this?/
Seriously, is that a joke?
Your infant daughter is sleeping/
Can you believe that she's still alive?
Her growing up with both parents/
Of that, she will be deprived
Enjoy your decapitation/ Please do not fret
This baby girl will awake to the sight
of your severed head inside of the bassinet
Reaping my rewards/ Life is golden and you have me sold
I'll snort a couple of lines of coke,
then one more for the road

INDECISIVE LOVE LETTER 2

First thing I want to see when I wake up
in the morning is your lovely face
Far be it from me to deprive you of sleep
in your eternal resting place
You deserve a day at the spa/
Get a massage, enjoy the sauna
Let's take a vacation in the Amazon/
You can go swimming and be devoured by piranha
Your elegance has left me speechless
and dumbfounded / What a wonder
Not a day goes by that I don't wish you six feet under
I've rented out an entire restaurant
for a private romantic dinner
Then we'll set sail on a yacht,
and I'll push you overboard/
Everyone is aware that you're not a very good swimmer
What I feel for you is all too real/
Here is a declaration of love on the spot
Pray my soul to keep, my hatred runs deep/
For you, I hope they keep Hell hot
Look at you with the appearance of a celestial being,
an astounding veritable angel
Do you want to see the inside of a hydraulic compacter?/
Investigators will find your body completely mangled
Take my hand and feel my warmth/
I want your body close
A heavy tool chest was dropped on top of your head/

It left you six weeks comatose
The tears you shed are that of joy/
I beg you not to cry
I'll fix you a drink, and make it a double of gin
and cyanide
You've always been a gorgeous lady,
looking even more stunning with each passing day
When you're in the sight of my M-16, I'll pull the trigger
without hesitation and spray
I feel like the luckiest man on earth
to have you by my side
Try this new moisturizer/ Apply it to your face/
It contains paint thinner and formaldehyde
There isn't anything in this world I would trade you for/
My one and only treasure
Strangling you with this slick,
silk scarf would be an absolute pleasure
The day that we met I must've had inside
of my pocket a four leaf clover
At the roof top bar there are sights to be seen
on the balcony ledge/
Hopefully you'll lose your balance and fall over
Come into my loving arms/ We'll dance the night away
Then with this gun I'll play a game of Safari/
I'm the hunter, you're the prey
Are you feeling comfortable and cozy while sitting with
me by the fireplace?
You'll be burned to ash/All remains will be removed,
acting only on instincts that are base

Oftentimes, I can see you in the night sky/ A magnificent rising star

I'll brain you then bag, and drag you all the way to be placed inside the trunk of my car

Our love is interwined along with our souls/ You dear, are my life

Cheese, pairing, or a cleaver/ I'm caring but carving/ I only require one knife

Perhaps we should purchase matching burial plots/ Forever together on an infinite vacation

Actually, I bought one with your name on it/ Already made reservations

I'm afraid I won't be joining you on this trip/ You'll be traveling alone

Your throat was slit just moments ago/ As a gentleman should, I'll escort you to your new home

EAT AT YOUR OWN RISK

Eat at your own risk/ We are serving lobster bisque
Turning pages of the menu/ Silence, listen to this!
Do you fancy Cajun Cuisine, a plate of fried alligator?
We'll serve you to the gators swimming out back/
Make a decision, it's now or later
Better believe none of us waiters are meek,
weak, or placid
Would you prefer to receive
in your face a splash of battery acid?
Stop complaining about our prices
before I draw my sword
and sever your vocal chords/ Is that something
you can afford?
Proud to be your waiter/ A professional mutilator
Chop up your thighs and serve them to patrons
with flavor they'll surely savor
At LeCuckold Restaurant, behold,
the presentation of superb dishes
Any negative feedback may result
in a deep sleep with the fishes
Seared scallops with pomegranate is the specialty
of the day
Dare to enter the kitchen to be maimed,
slayed and filleted?
So pleased that you decided to stay/ Hey, and by the way

Order something then send it back
to the chef if you want to play
However, that is highly unrecommended/
He'll be indubitably offended
A master chef with above average culinary skills/ He has
transcended
Above and beyond/Make a selection arbitrarily or otherwise
Demonstrating uncouth behavior could lead to an
early demise
Observe how the chocolate souffle flows
Goes well served with wine after eating some escargot
Can't help but remember a patron
from earlier in the day
He was also indecisive but eventually
ordered roast duck flambé
What a nice suit that he wore/
I spilled wine all over it with shame
Then I threw the flambé into his lap,
which was soon engulfed in flames
The patron got up and ran straight into the kitchen
Who knows what he did that for?/
All he needed was a mortician
Screaming incoherently isn't something
that will alleviate the situation
The chef beat the patron with a meat tenderizer,
giving way to proper persuasion
The kitchen crew extinguished the flames
of this burning corpse
Now it's time for you to order/

Let's start with the main course
Beef Burgundy, what a delightful choice/
I forgot to bring the wine list
I'll bring you a glass of Dom Perignon on the house/
Yes, I must insist
Twenty minutes have passed/
You're famished and ready to eat
Here is the beef stew and wine
with a complimentary salad, bon appetite
Glad that you're enjoying your dinner/
What we serve here is pure ambrosia
Dishes of heavenly delight/
Out of sight, take a moment to smell the aroma
The finest in French cuisine/ It'll bring you to your knees
Did I mention that the chef was kind enough
to add to the stew some anti freeze?
At least your meal is finished,
and now you've paid your penance
Try not to worry, It'll all be over in a minute
Here comes the part when you struggle
to breathe and clutch your chest
Hopefully after your reincarnation
you'll dine here once again with the very best

THE ROAD TO RUSSIAN ROULETTE

Gentlemen, please sit down at the table
in your assigned seats
The four of you will now experience a tremendous treat
Special arrangements were made
with such precision and care
I do apologize that all participants
were required to strip down to their underwear
At first you all needed a little convincing
by my associate with his assault rifle
Your defiance quickly ceased/
In fact, all forms of protest were stifled
Harsher tactics can be a necessity in life,
and it's categorically a shame
When my only intention is for us to get together
and simply play a game
Welcome to my recreation room,
Woodrow, Lance, Chuck, and Samson
We're here to have a good time only/
Rest assure, you're not being held for ransom
Chuck, do you remember in the second grade
when you played with some of my clay?
Later, I asked for it back/ You shook your head and told
me to have a nice day
After that refusal, you and your buddies here
became incredibly brutal

I got the "filling" beaten out of me as
if I were strawberry strudel
Some would say, I should forgive and move on/
That's what retribution is for
You might've noticed several armed associates of mine,
guarding the exit doors
Regrettably, I'm without hors d'oeuvres
and wine to serve, as each one of you sits in a chair
Soon this'll be the least of your concerns
after I provide much more than you can possibly bear
I'm more than confident that all participants
of this game will learn a valuable lesson
Oh, what fun it is to play
with a six shot Smith and Wesson
The gun has been placed in the middle of the table/
Be careful when you aim and shoot it
If any attempts are made to end my life,
you're guaranteed to be executed
One of the players has a legitimate
chance of walking away/
Do You feel any remorse or regret?
Be sure to have fun and enjoy yourselves
while playing this enthralling game of Russian Roulette
Lance was first to try his luck/ He seemed so full of anger
People tend to realize just how precious life
is when there's a bullet loaded in the chamber
The cylinder of the gun was spun around,
before Lance pressed the muzzle against his own head
Sweat poured profusely from his brow,

while filled with an overwhelming sense of dread
Emotions such as fear permeated this group/
I struggled to suppress my laughter and sniggered
A sigh of relief is what Lance had taken
after pulling the trigger
"Lady Luck" didn't shine as bright on Chuck/
Unfortunately as he feared
After pulling the trigger a bullet came forth,
piercing Chuck ear to ear
His body quickly collapsed onto the floor,
as the bullet ricocheted off the wall
It was time to make this game a little more exciting/
Indeed I had the gall
To refill the gun with five bullets instead of one/
Soon I'll set another contestant "free"
Too much time has been taken to kill these cunts/
It was beginning to trigger my ADHD
Samson was famished/ He wished to stop playing
preferably to eat some soup and bread
I ordered him to place the barrel
of the gun inside his mouth/He was fed hot lead instead
The trigger was pulled
and the bullet blew out the back of Samson's head
Although I wasn't sufficiently satisfied/
How amusing, "That's what she said"
Woodrow had taken a turn/ No bullet for him/
Now it's back to Lance
Perhaps he'll survive two rounds in a row/
There's only a minimal chance

I spun the cylinder then gave the gun back to Lance/
My instructions were the same and plain
Lance pulled the trigger of this Smith and Wesson
and blew out his own brains
My associates and I cheered while praising
Woodrow, declaring him the winner of our game
Apparently Woodrow wasn't thrilled to be alive/
He said, that I am utterly insane
The ability to breathe is the greatest award bestowed,
but now I wanted this man far from my sight
In my heart I knew Woodrow didn't deserve to live,
so I waved at him and said, "Nighty night"
I filled every chamber of that revolver/
Then proceeded in shooting His body
Woodrow stood up and "danced"
after receiving each bullet,
making him the life of the party
He was the last man at this event to die
and that he did, which left me hypnotized
Woodrow chose not to walk away as the winner,
but did receive a consolation prize

CARNAGE SERVED WITH A SMILE

This you cannot believe/ Look at this delectable cuisine
Eat well and fill your belly/
Feel free to indulge is what I mean
Over all the food is inexpensive/ This is just a local diner
Frida's the best waitress around/
There is no one else who is kinder
Alas, not anymore/ Now she has a bone to pick
Grievances lead to malfeasance/
Customers are making her sick
Her loving boyfriend, Jacob has bolted the door
Wait till you hear what she eagerly has in store
Gratuitous violence will ensue/
The type that chills you to the core
Enticing executions bestowed raw/
More morbid ambition to explore
Frida asked, "Who thinks
I can live on these measly inadequate tips?
What my boss calls a salary are scraps and crumbs/
Nothing more than insignificant tidbits
Not gently, I'm presenting justice/
Won't stop until I bypass all hindrance
Better than apple pie/
Best dish served cold is a heaping amount of vengeance
Add plenty of whip cream/ Place a cherry on top
Don't bother screaming for help,

and no one's calling the cops
Thank you for all of your patronage,
but all penny pinchers must die
On the floor, in no time at all,
is where your bodies will lie"
Jacob used an uzi to shoot someone
that was sitting at a table
Earlier, this patron complained
because Frida didn't serve along
with his pancakes, syrup that was flavored maple
The young waitress held in her hand a 357 revolver
There isn't anything that this gun can't handle/
A reliable problem solver
The manager was in his office/
Frida wanted him to be aware of the matter
She went back there and pulled the trigger/
The manager's brains were splattered
All over the wall which recently received
a fresh coat of paint
He was oblivious to what was going on
but he was hardly a saint
Refusing to give Frida a raise is unreasonable,
especially after all this time
Three years and counting, this is why the server found
it suitable to blow the manager's mind
In a world so cruel, Frida didn't have any compunction
regarding what she did/
This is precisely how she functions
Frida emerged from the office/

She approached Jacob and gave him a kiss
Then looked deeply into his eyes,
which brought her contentment and bliss
The server appeared imperious,
ruling by the side of her man
Jacob had a second uzi/
He placed it in the palm of Frida's hand
My, oh, my, what a day/
During these precious moments they slay
The couple with itchy trigger fingers allowed
their bullets to spray
Seventeen dead, no one in the diner was spared/
Lives were taken with flair
The killers danced around
the dead bodies like Ginger Rogers and Fred Astaire
The time had come to take their exit/
Police sirens are what they heard
Dancing to the tune of this quaint little diner massacre

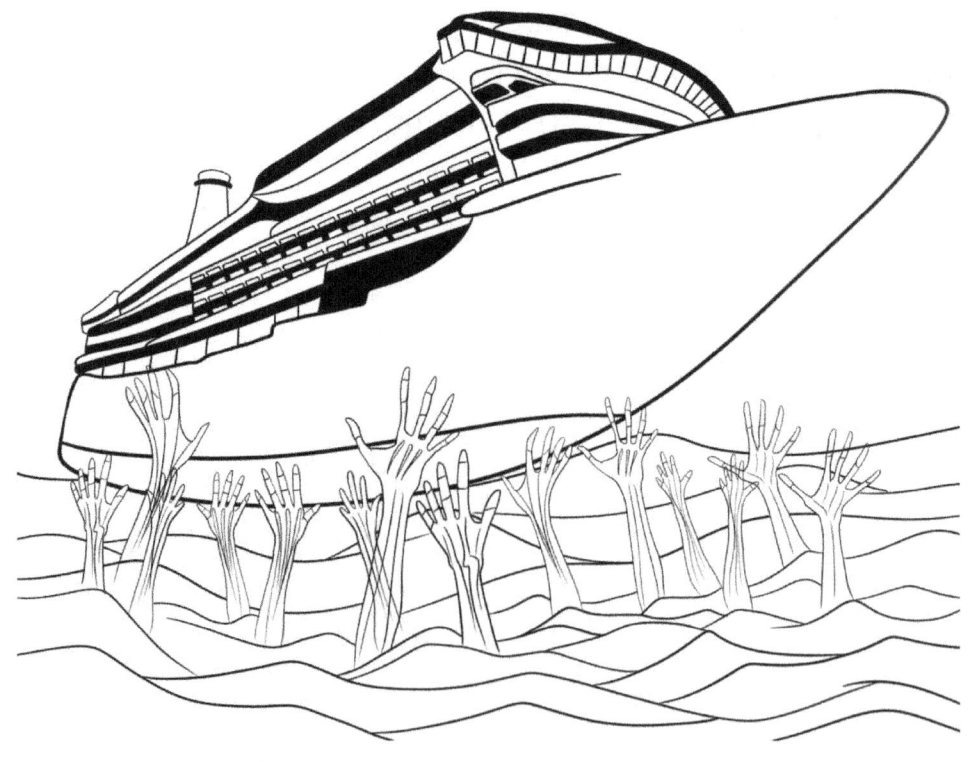

SET SAIL FOR HELL

Good day, me maties and I just boarded this cruise ship
Excuse me, sir/
Do you have any chips to go along with this dip?
Can't wait to check out all of the amenities
of this vessel within the vicinity
Minature golf, night clubs, and bars/
Are you kidding me?
Racing to rate the rave/ What is it that I crave?
We harness the carnage/
So, severely deranged and depraved
Redrum is in the air with flair/ Can you feel it?
Plunder and pillage, running amok/
We welcome with open arms blood spillage
A true testament to my malevolence/
Evident with all excellence
Capable of taking more lives than pestilence
Believe me when I say, this message comes straight
from the heart
In consideration of fair play,
passengers will be getting a head start
There's eight of us now on board/
No hesitation to draw our swords
Guaranteed to lead to disembowelments/
Bodies will hit the floor
We all went to the bar to imbibe
the beer that's been brewed
There we encountered Dougie, Stanley, Sammie and Rue

Stanley didn't smoke cigars or pipes/ He preferred to use vapor
His demeanor was smug, so me matey sodomized him
with a sabre
Right up the rectum and straight through the mouth
Pictures were taken as proof to dissuade any doubt
Besides, this forged a beautiful memory/
When all else fails
Hijack a ship with your maties and set sail for Hell
Thanks to Stanley's haughty,
uppity attitude, he's been laid to rest
Sammie suffered a fatal sabre wound directly
through her chest
Me maties and I drank more and sang songs/
Passengers were ordered to sing along
Rue sung a song off key with a screech/
Not much effort applied which is wrong
Suddenly, a matey grabbed Rue by the hair,
and dragged her across the deck
Please, no judgment, we're all pirates/
What did you really expect?
In the old days she would've been forced
to walk the plank, which we all adore
There wasn't any time for formalities,
so Rue was thrown overboard
That poor woman in the freezing ocean/
I wish it could be hotter
At least she won't die alone,
because it's known that sharks inhabit these waters
Cannot jump up and down on the bed as a child/

You must lie down instead
It wasn't long before a school of Caribbean reef sharks
ripped through Rue like lightly toasted bread
What a bloody relief that this wench is dead
Rue never seized an opportunity to strive in life,
but at least the fishes are fed
Oops, I mean sharks/ Hark, someone is playing the harp
Passenger cabins were looted while listening to music/
That's the most soothing part
Dougie was decapitated, because of this his wife
Trudy insulted my eye patch
Subsequently, I pushed her to the floor,
then used my peg leg to step in her snatch
Trudy let loose a high pitched scream,
as she stuck up her middle finger
It was two octaves higher than a soprano
or any kind of opera singer
Then I used a knife to remove her eyes,
so she can sympathize
With those out there that cannot see/
Her poor judgment must be realized
Any acknowledgement at all will do/
A perfect lesson for me to give
Due to massive blood loss from in between
Trudy's legs, she didn't have long to live
Most of the passengers have been savagely murdered,
with our anger directed at the source
We certainly plundered, the seven seas are a wonder/
Time for us to set a new course

THE CHURCH OF REPERCUSSIONS

On Sunday morning, Minister Hines greeted his congre-
gation, with brethren as far as the eye can see
In this church there is never any shortage of hypocrisy
There are degenerate gamblers, gold diggers,
and lushes in full stock
Men that cheat on their wives, hussies,
and drug addicts/ What an inspiring flock
Donations are always accepted/
The minister fills his pockets to the brim
The church always passes compliance audits,
so he's guaranteed to do it again
A follower donated $20,000 in exchange for a miracle
After learning the details of this transaction
can you blame people for being cynical?
His wife had stage four cancer of the larynx,
which caused her to lose her voice
Instead, the funds were used as a down payment
for the minister's Rolls Royce
Such a joyous occasion with everyone attending mass/
Now there will be mass murder
In quantities and volumes never heard of/
Today Glenn Ruskins will be the "sheep herder"
He carried with him a laundry bag,
but instead of clothes it contained tools
Such as the handgun used to rob parishioners,

and alleviate them from bracelets and jewels
Gold watches and necklaces were on the list/
Can't forget about the diamond rings
This caused more than enough chaos
to make the choir want to sing
Are you all oblivious to what you've done?/
Be prepared to compensate
With an axe hand, Glenn decapitated Landro Rollins/
His head rolled onto the collection plate
One woman claimed that she received the holy ghost,
seemed as though she was having a seizure
A trembling delight for a man to bring home to mother/
Yeah, she's a real keeper
The minister placed a wafer inside of a parishioner's
mouth, and said, "Accept the body of Christ"
Ruskins approached Hines then slapped him in the
mouth/ He said, "It's best to take your own advice"
Glenn asked the entire congregation,
"What is it that you all wish for?
Don't be coy, go ahead and answer, by the way,
I chained the door"
Guess what was hidden underneath one of the pews?/
It happened to be a cross bow
There are an abundance of arrows to give,
and the good book teaches that the
insolent will reap what they sow
Minister Hines presented blood of Christ in the form of
wine but there wasn't a lot
Glenn demanded another bottle after

he finished having four shots
Ruskins stroked his firearm/
Hine's flock thought Glenn had been possessed
Then a young man was shot through the heart/
Should've prayed for a bulletproof vest
Mr. Towers got down on his knees to pray/
The cold air caused him to shiver
Glenn was pleased that the old man got
his two cents in before he pulled the trigger
After killing several people in the choir,
Ruskins doused Hines with wine from an open bottle
Then Glenn said, "Truth be told, this'll be rough/
You will not be coddled"
A match was struck and a fire ignited/
Screams from the flock all sounded the same
Why were they making so much racket?/
The minister is the only one writhing in pain
Although there were cooler autumn nights
and days, Hines had been set ablaze
Seems that clergymen being burned
alive is now all the rave
Turns out that Minister Hines is the greatest heathen/
His flock is currently seeing
A smoldering cadaver, center stage/
This sight is certainly worth believing
Hines is now in the afterlife/
It was Glenn's pleasure to send him there
Purgatory or straight to Hell/
The sinful must not be spared

Ruskins prepared to take his leave,
then told everyone to stay and remain calm
Glenn ran in stride after leaving a donation of his own,
which was a delay-action bomb
Subsequently, the church was blown
to bits along with the brethren within
There are dire consequences for one's egregious actions/
All of the parishioners paid for their sins

HUSBANDS ARE LACTOSE INTOLERANT

The year is 1948 and I don't want to be late
I'm a milk man with an overwhelming
amount of deliveries to make
When the cat is away the mice can't help but to play
Today is the day and I'm dazed with quite a few dates
Bottles of milk are not free as I aim to please
Sexual appetites and needs to appease/ It's like a disease
While the husbands are at work it's my job to swoop in
To make every single delivery again and again
At the Palmer's residence,
the lady of the house wished to receive her milk
She answered the door wearing lingerie as smooth as silk
Presumably, that was material it was made from,
or perhaps satin weave
There's something from the bedroom
that Mrs. Palmer wished for me to retrieve
It's my obligation to comply, then the deed was done
With more deliveries to make, my apologies,
now I must run
Before I could depart, guess who decided to show?
The man of the house/ Well, what do you know?
Mr. Palmer was not pleased, as a military great
A veteran that's still in possession of his Walther P-38
Which he pulled out to shoot, so I zigged and zagged
Before leaping through a window to avoid getting tagged

Thank goodness we were on the first floor
Here comes Mr. Palmer charging out the backdoor
His finger on the trigger of a gun that's cocked
Fiercely shooting while chasing me
all the way down the block
After entering someone's yard I picked up a rake
I'll choose my personal safety
over the husband's life that I must take
Made it around the side of this house/
Palmer continued to pursue
Cannot allow trepidation to overcome
when you know what to do
As soon as Palmer stepped around the corner,
I hit him in the head with enough space
A soldier that had been honorably
discharged is now a disgrace
I quickly lunged for the gun,
and removed it from Palmer's grasp
Then shot him in the neck which bloodied the grass
Right then and there, Palmer dropped dead,
so I went ahead
Back on my delivery route
with many more women to bed
Later on, a lady's husband came home early/
Caught me in the middle of third base
Already with a double barrel shotgun in hand,
he pulled the trigger and blew off my face

DISPICABLE DREAMS

Deep down in my dreams
I'll emerge triumphant and score
Allow us to reach new heights/
Destined to ascend and soar
Leave poverty far behind/
An embarrassing abysmal economical stain
Success is within grasp/
Riches and fame are mine to claim
Courtney and I shall finally be married
after three years of dating/ She's the girl of my dreams
Having ownership of beachfront
property with scenery so serene
All ailments and illnesses will dissipate/
Imagine a cure for cancer discovery
Everyone currently plagued will go into remission
and immediate recovery
Little Rita, wipe away those tears/ Why do you cry?
It's a monumental gift just to be here alive
Do you hear the cheers from children
playing in the street?
If world peace can be achieved that'll be an amazing feat
The most magnificent event on earth
to observe is a sunrise
Sunsets are equally captivating
even when merged with city skylines
There is an abundance of beauty to behold/
Some of which has never been seen

by the human eye/
Hopefully not confined to my wildest dreams...
In actuality it's time for a reality check
Little Rita is a local pick pocket
that almost stole my wallet, so I snapped her neck
My Uncle Morty has stage three cancer/
He molested me since the age of three
Hope he doesn't survive/ Hurry up and die/
I'll feel so liberated and free
My next door neighbor,
Gaspar allowed his dog to defecate in my yard
One morning, I went out onto my porch
and stepped in it/ Now he has gone too far
Through vindictive devices
I had to make Gaspar see the error of his ways
Very little effort on my part is required
but that bastard must pay
I fed his dog a well cooked pork chop,
laced with a poisonous pesticide
The animal soon dropped dead,
and with it I felt a tremendous sense of pride
I knocked on Gaspar's front door then he answered,
invited me in for some tea
Of course I accepted then entered
the humble abode, being both deceitful and crafty
by taking initiative and insisting
on preparing my own blend of tea that I brought along
Gaspar sat down in the living room,
patiently waiting while listening to his favorite song

With haste, the tea has been produced
and served in the dining room
My cup only contained water,
which my neighbor would learn all too soon
Not long after consuming the beverage,
Gaspar lost his sense of vision
Quite a story that there was to tell,
so I gave him my admission
I said, "You were told not to allow your dog
to shit in my yard, if you recall
This happened on several different occasions
and you didn't listen, always walking tall
The price you pay for your transgressions is damage to
your retinas/ retinal
This little miracle is made possible
by consuming large quantities of methanol
Now I know that you might be upset right now
and think that I Should go to jail
But imagine all the fun you'll have learning
how to read using braille"
Gaspar screamed at the top of his lungs,
as I merrily skipped all the way home
Despite obscenities coming from my neighbor's mouth,
and I really didn't like his tone
I found my beautiful fiance,
Courtney taking a bubble bath
Getting ready for a night on the town,
but I have reasons to obstruct her path
Courtney considered it odd

that I stood before her and simply stared
This woman does whatever she chooses/
We made such a pair
She thinks that I'm oblivious to her illicit affair
That's been going on with Gaspar of all people/
Now it wouldn't be fair
If my fiance didn't also answer for her insipid offenses
No one can merely coast through life/
There will always be consequences
I picked up my lady's curling iron/
It was already plugged in
Let's exhibit the courage to enable
the power of healing to begin
I dropped the device in the water,
and Courtney was electrocuted
It turns out she's a perfect match for Gaspar
with a fate very well suited
It's in my best interest to go back
and finish my neighbor off
I'll probably stomp his head in and scream out, mazeltov!

YOU LIGHT MY FUSE

What an astounding day/ Shimney O'Brien wished he
was a member of the IRA
Not because he cared for the cause,
or wished for the British to pay
As a fanatical fellow that's resilient and tough
He's a ticking time bomb obsessed with blowing stuff up
At the local bakery the cashier named
Shelly refused to give O'Brien his change
She huffed before walking away from the register/
This behavior is a tad strange
Shimney took a bite of his cupcake
before walking out the front door
The only remedy for a lack of manners
is properly planted C-4
There weren't any perceptible witnesses,
so Shimney reached into his backpack
in order for him to exact revenge subsequent
to finishing his snack
The impertinence of that employee caused
O'Brien to cringe
Justice will be served after blowing
this bakery back to Stonehenge
Suddenly, O'Brien retracted his tactics/
This is going too far
Why destroy a lovely confectionary shop
when a device can be placed underneath Shelly's car?
Shimney had seen her before/

He knows which automobile she drives
The world will be much more pleasant
when Shelly ceases to be alive
Explosives were set strategically/
O'Brien was in close enough range and proximity
An astounding event to bear witness to,
and for all gazers within the vicinity
Time passed before Shelly came out into the parking lot/
It must be time for her break
Soon she'll be behind the wheel
without knowing what's at stake
Shiney thought, "Such a hapless harpy/
Don't forget to say, bye-bye to all of your friends
With that attitude, I doubt they have any desire
to ever see you again
Valid mistakes can be forgiven,
but you're a petty, puny crumb
Your life has little meaning and even less value/
Three whole dollars is the sum
That's the amount in change,
you failed to give back/ Therefore, you're a thief
This'll be the longest lunch break you ever had/
I grant you eternal sleep
Have a seat and put on your safety belt/
Better safe than sorry
Once you've been blown sky high
I'll pop some champagne/
Fiesta, it's time to party!
Shelly, are you ready to drive away?/

There will not be any procrastination
One, for the ugly/ Two, for your face/
It's time for remote detonation"
Shimney hit the switch and the explosives blew/
Hallelujah, give him praise
Pieces of Shelly were everywhere/
Sanitation workers will be picking her up for days
During all the chaos that ensued
O'Brien wisely vacated the scene
This catastrophe could've been averted simply
by not being mean

THE PUTRID ODOR OF LOVE

Young students must acquire education
and knowledge is power
The quantity of ill-informed citizens
seems to increase by the hour
Lina Danvers' job is to educate, embolden,
and mold developing minds
into pillars of society that will fall in line
with what's expected of them/
Mrs. Danvers cannot easily be fooled
She's a biology teacher at the local high school
Necessity comes at a cost/ There's a line that she crossed
After becoming smitten
with a sixteen year old student named Mark LeMoss
Lina didn't consider herself much older/
She was only thirty-eight
In her mind there isn't any such thing as statutory rape
There had been multiple rendezvous between the lustful
teacher and Mark
Lina will not be denied/
Her desires so dark, yet vivid and stark
Mrs. Danvers broke her vows/
She has been married for the past six years
She slit her husband's throat in his sleep
and didn't shed a tear
This outcome is an occurrence
that her ill-fated partner had inadvertently forced
He didn't allow for nature to take its inevitable course

This teacher rode haughtily on her high horse/
Some people may wonder, why?
The heart wants what it wants/
Lina continued to hold her head up high
Her husband discovered that she was having an affair/
Put an end to it?/ Never!
Lina loved Mark and wished to be
with him forever and ever
Rumors began to circulate at school,
and they must be addressed
A meeting with the principal
and superintendent had been
scheduled which caused Lina great distress
The night before this assembly
Mrs. Danvers took time to reflect
As she minutely examined the deep knife
wound on her deceased husband's neck
Lina thought to herself, "If I go to jail will,
'Lost in love' be the charge?"
After dragging her husband to the bathtub,
and placing him inside, Lina began to carve
Last year for a Christmas present,
Mr. Danvers gave his wife a set
of brand new kitchen knives
In retrospective it certainly seems
that this gift selection was entirely unwise
The next morning,
Mrs. Danvers was punctual in greeting the
principal and superintendent

She apologized but said,
all of the claims were false/ So,
no one should feel offended
However, the principal didn't believe a word,
and she told Lina that she was fired
Lina lost her composure, glared at the principal,
before screaming, "You're the liar!"
The superintendent decided to intervene and said,
"Let's not make this any worse"
Mrs. Danvers calmed herself, and cracked
a smile before reaching into her purse
A Saturday Night Special was pulled forth/
Both the superintendent and principal
were caught by surprise
After the trigger was rapidly tapped,
on the floor is where these faculty members died
With a smug sense of satisfaction,
Mrs. Danvers went to class and retrieved Mark
The student that satiated all of Lina's needs/
They were to never be apart
They both left the school,
and got inside of Lina's car for one final act
When Mrs. Danvers shows up on the doorstep of
Mark's parents, how will they react?
Mr. and Mrs. LeMoss would never approve of
Mark and Lina's union/
Their love will quickly be debunked
This is why after arriving at the house,
Mrs. Danvers immediately

Acquired a tool from her trunk
Denouncing the future of these lovebirds
is what the LeMosses are bound to do/
This is not conjecture
Mark rung the doorbell as Lina hid
a double-bit axe behind her back for good measure
Mrs. Danvers stood there with Mark by her side,
eagerly determined
The front door was answered
with a blast from an elephant gun
straight through Lina's sternum
Mr. LeMoss ordered his son
to march upstairs to his room
Mark pouted but did what he was told,
as his beloved's death loomed
The teacher's chest cavity had been exposed/
Mr. LeMoss stared down at the ground
Lina struggled to catch her breath until
she no longer could,
despite her love that was so profound

ASPIRATIONS
OF AN ARSONIST 2

Pappa's playing the piano in the den,
and it makes me want to start a fire
Passion and pain are burning deep inside/
My chest is bound to burst with desire
Have you ever seen a man screaming
while running about,
with his entire body engulfed in flames?
That's the type of love that I'm compelled to give/
I wonder if you're willing to do the same
Don't fight, I'll ignite it with a single match in hand
You can burn rapidly, not happily,
because I really don't give damn
Pappa's gone now/ I don't know
what to do beside setting anotherfire
The building down the street has some problems
with their electrical work/
Perhaps I'll play with some loose wires
Am I severely lacking compassion?/
But I'm splashing kerosene on the floor
Only a gallon was utilized,
I think it needs a little more
My conscience is something
for the very first time that should be deeply explored
Then again, Mrs. Tiddleman is up in age/
Hopefully her cries for help will be ignored

It isn't anything personal against her really/
Our personalities don't even clash
Regardless, I deem it suitable
for Tiddleman along with her house
to be vastly reduced to ash
This is just my neighborly way of saying,
hello, or giving an egregious goodbye
Branches from her tree have been hanging over
my property line/ That's a good enough reason, why
To forsake and bake her into a souffle/
Not to be eaten but merely discarded
These are the events that occasionally take place/
It's enough to leave me disheartened
Although if it does, it never lasts long/
Never give up hope
It warms my heart much like a house
when it's filled with smoke
The fire gave Mrs. Tiddleman a drastic makeover
that caused her face to melt
Soon her husband will return home to an unpleasant
surprise / A sense of accomplishment is what I felt
Loving thy neighbors/ Breaking bread with enemies
Until they're all burnt to a crisp,
posterity is brought forth by these sweet memories
It turned out that Mrs. Tiddleman's ailing
mother is also home
Both women continue to roast,
as they remain in the danger zone
I'm feeling giddy as I giggle

while watching these two women sizzle,
inside of their own homestead as
if their bodies were on the griddle
Damn, these flames are burning bright/
Is this house built of bricks or wicker?
The husband finally arrived home/
To my own bewilderment he began to snicker
Mr. Tiddleman actually hated his wife
and mother-in-law/ Turns out, I did him a favor
Women revel in divorce settlements that take place in
California/Making me Jesus Christ, his savior
911 was called over twenty minutes ago/
The fire trucks still haven't arrived
I joined Mr. Tiddleman outside
to make some smores, and we gave each other high fives

Breaking News

NEWS AT 11

Good evening, this is Channel 18 news/
I'm Robert T. Hayes with Tabitha Lorrel
Fasten your seatbelts and tune
in for a joyride straight through hell
At approximately four this afternoon
there was a road rage incident
Between an elderly man identified as Kevin Terrent
The other participant instigated/
A young man named Stan Hoag
He found it amusing to cut Terrent off,
and damn near ran him off of the road
Despite feeling discombobulated,
Terrent observed Stan sitting at a red light
Kevin Terrent happened to be a Vietnam vet/
Hoag probably should've said, goodnight
Stan sped off without a moment's notice
as soon as the light turned green
Terrent pulled out his old sniper rifle now adapted
with an infrared beam
Stan the man tried to close his jacket,
but his sleeve got caught in the zipper
While distracted, a couple of slow breaths were taken by
an old pro then Terrent pulled the trigger
Problem solving is Stan's specialty
but it was Terrent that blew his mind
When investigators arrived
and examined the victim's dashboard,

Hoag's brains were quite the find
A negative reaction is what Stan was searching
for and ultimately made amends
By forfeiting his life/ Cutting off a driver in traffic/
He'll never make that mistake again
This just in, a woman almost got car jacked
at a local gas station
Armed with a .45, she blew a hole through
the assailant's chest/
Now bound to become an internet sensation
Membrance Bank, branch at 16th
and Homer was robbed by an unorthodox crew
They didn't make demands for cash,
but requests/ People heard a lot of please and thank you
The majority of the money was meant
for the robbers to take,
but account holders didn't know what to do
When one of the gun men stuck stacks
of hundred dollar bills into
their pockets, and wished for all of their dreams
to come true
Eventually, the robbers were taken into custody/
Two of them were shot dead on the spot
Then the authorities confiscated
money from customers/
Now, who actually should've been laid to rot?
Victoria Shevon had been bamboozled
by a reverse mortgage scheme
An elderly woman that was well respected in town

and held in high esteem
She was too old to start all over,
and couldn't afford to lose her home
Shevon loaded her deceased husband's hunting rifle
and 9mm Beretta that's chrome
Then she got dressed
and drove ten miles directly to the business
That eagerly seeked to make her homeless/
What kind of people could do this?
She marched into Dandro's Reverse
Mortgage company building and wanted to see the man
Responsible for all of her stress,
this is not a request, but indubitably a demand
The associate that she signed the contract with appeared
This man seemed sorrowful and on the verge of tears
Victoria counted fifteen other employees/
Men and women that were currently present
All working to get rich by stealing more homes from
"The peasants"
Victoria said, "None of you are the least bit ethical, or
show any signs of virtue
But don't worry your pretty little heads/
I know exactly what to do"
Already with a rifle in her hands,
Victoria began taking shots
Only two escaped/ Fourteen cadavers discovered
by the cops/ Oh, my, that's a lot
Now, you the viewers might be wondering,
why I'm stabbing Tabitha, my co-host?

She's getting an executive position even though
I'm much more
charismatic and deserving of the post
Tabitha, you can attempt to struggle as a damsel in dis-
tress, but allow me to be blunt
Corporate promised me a higher salary,
you pretentious little cunt
Guess you won't be getting that promotion after all/
Cry, boo hoo and sing the blues
I might be going to jail but for a while I'll be the biggest
story on the news
Lorrel is not doing well, in fact she's dead,
however I'm still on a winning streak
In handcuffs, I can still stand tall
with my imminent bonus/
Don't you know that it's Sweeps Week?

PROSTITUTES MAKE THE WORLD GO ROUND

There is a busy harlot named Debra
that is more than efficient at turning tricks
She love you long time, but be careful she'll get you sick
Exposed to all sorts of ailments/
I regret to inform you it's not the flu
Placed a hex with voodoo/
Do what you do to avoid that bad juju
Harold Brentons had a good time
and left but Debra wasn't paid
A year later, Brenton had a blood test,
then he was diagnosed as having full blown AIDS
Last night Jerome picked up the working girl
in his automobile
Drove out to Fulton Point to park
after treating her to a fine meal
High quality attire is what this man wore with pizzazz
Debra pulled a pistol from her purse,
and attempted to rob the gentleman for all of his cash
Natural rebellion caused Jerome to make a mistake,
and reach for the gun instead
With much vigor and conviction the trigger was pulled,
and Jerome received a bullet to the head
Debra vacated the automobile and left the gun/
This incident left her emotionally spent and tired
It was getting late/ Just for shits and giggles,

she set the car on fire
All of Jerome's hopes and dreams were going up in smoke
At least the contents of his wallet had been
"bequeathed" to Debra which made it easier to cope
This sudden loss is a tragedy/ A valid stud of valor
Thank goodness that she brought a gun of this caliber
Ambition to sleep her way to the top/
Time to give it a rest
Chicken is not for sale, but here are two legs,
thighs, and breasts
Guaranteed to do anything for you that pleases
The perfect whore if you eagerly seek
to contract venereal diseases
What's the matter?/
Does your pee pee burn while urinating?/
The message is well written
Gonorrhea is the perfect gift/
So glad to you that it was given
Consider yourself a lucky man
and know that you'll have a blast
After discovering that your pubic hair
is now infested with crabs
One day a John named Don refused to pay,
and told Debra not to get her panties in a bunch
This crude remark was followed
by an unkind gesture that came in the form of a punch
This harsh treatment went on for a while,
so long/ Don was late for a meeting
It can be said by any witness,

that Debra had taken one helluva beating
Then she decided to apologize and offer further service
Don was pleasantly surprised Debra had learned her place, and decided to be more courteous
Passionate kisses were given by the working girl, while stroking her attacker's penis
Don said, "I'm glad that we were able to reconcile without any animosity between us"
He was from an affluent walk of life, and the working girl is straight from the gutter
The kissing diversion was more than adequate, as Debra pulled out her box cutter
She used it to make a large gash across Don's neck/ He covered the gaping wound as well as he could
Then Debra proceeded in working her magic to remove a curse known as Don's manhood
Such shrills/ A tourniquet and medical treatment is what the John immediately needed
Debra grinned with glee, as the flustered John desperately begged and pleaded
Tears flowed like a river from Don's eyes as he screamed, "Do your worst!"
The vengeful woman replied, "I already did by removing your bratwurst
Now give me all of your cash and credit cards/ You may feel compelled to shout
But I'll call a taxi cab for myself/ You'll be too busy bleeding out
The next morning, a jogger discovered the grisly scene,

which is enough to drive a man to drink
It's time for breakfast/
How about eggs and bacon, but where is
Don's missing sausage link?

MASTER OF WILD KINGDOM

Beware of Cliff the professional dog walker/
He takes strolls down the street
He saw Ben approaching from the opposite direction,
so he unhooked the pitbull from his leash
The poor man ran at full speed while being chased/
This never should've been allowed
That pit bull had his way with Ben
by turning him into puppy chow
Cliff stood idly by and assured his victim
that this dog doesn't actually bite
This absurd statement fell on deaf ears/
Ben wasn't putting up much of a fight
It's difficult to do so when you've already met
your demise/ Cliff and the dog began to walk south
Ben had been reduced to chunks
with a piece of his chin inside of the pit bull's mouth
One afternoon, Cliff decided to visit the local zoo
He observed the lion's exhibit
and didn't know what to do
A large sign had been posted above the animals' den
Cliff read, "Please do not feed"/ This sentiment didn't
sit right with him
He never believed that humans
should hold dominion over what animals eat
Lions don't shop at grocery stores/

They're carnivores and in desperate need of raw meat
The young man became exceedingly
agitated after reading the sign again
His impulses were no longer kept under control,
so he pushed an unsuspecting woman in
Roxy is her name and the predicament was fraught,
but precisely what Cliff sought
The pursuit persisted with this woman on the run/
Soon enough she'll be caught
Two lions from the pack were after Roxy/
The both bit her on opposite ends
of her body/ So tragic, unreal just like magic/
This is where the fun really begins
Roxy was torn in half and eviscerated
with her intestines spilling out onto the ground
All her screams were deafening
until she ceased to utter a sound
Despite being displaced from their natural habitat,
these majestic beasts eat well with prime beef cuts
All the lion cubs also had their fill from feeding on
Roxy's guts
Spectators at the exhibit bellowed in horror/
They couldn't believe what they beared witness to
With Cliff around you're bound
to have one helluva time at the zoo
Our anti hero was feeling quite duplicitous/
Up in the night sky you can see the moon
An arrangement had been made for Cliff
to receive a shipment of feisty, rabid raccoons

At approximately 7:30 -8:00 pm his neighbor,
Grant brings out to the dumpster all of his trash
The raccoons were let loose only minutes before/
The lid was shut on Grant's behalf
Cliff's neighbor made his appearance right on time,
precisely in the exact place
The dumpster lid was lifted up/
Then a raccoon latched on to Grant's face
His shrieks were profoundly muffled,
as three more raccoons were on the attack
They've been starving for several days,
and in dire need of more than a snack
Teeth and claws were embedded
and shredded flesh in an adequate food source
Today is certainly not Grant's lucky day
after becoming tonight's main course
Investigators didn't find
any evidence of Cliff's involvement/
His plan was diabolical
Eventually, a funeral service for Grant was held,
closed casket of course,
because the raccoons left him unrecognizable

HAPPY ABORTION ON ARBOR'S DAY

Vroom, vroom, Welcome to the clinic
on this glorious day
What were the circumstances that compelled
you to stifle a life today?
You're not required to give a reason
if it's your preference not to say
An ample amount of women are here
with many more on the way
Some people refer to us as apostates that follow heresy
We're doing the Lord's work
by getting rid of unwanted pregnancies
Smile, because you won't be giving birth/
We'll discard what's inside
Put your feet up in those stirrups and open wide
If you laid eyes on our medical waste
it would cause you to chuck
But your vomit just like all these fetuses
we hastily vacuum up
Vroom, vroom/ We'll do our best to keep
this theme in tune
You're thinking, hurry
and get this thing out of my womb
Peppermint patties, if your clothes are ratty
then it is time for a change
Women not having control over their own bodies/

A concept that is completely deranged
Thanks to Roe V. Wade being overturned,
men will make the decision for you which sounds insane
Pluck this unwanted seed from my snatch/
For you, I'll gladly do the same
If a girl is raped and impregnated
by the ripe old age of thirteen
Should she be forced to have that baby?/
Do you know what this means?
That young girl and her rapist's offspring, together/
Seems like quite a team
Everytime she looks into the eyes of that infant,
it makes her want to scream
Coincidentally, this happened to Ashley
and she was forced to have a baby boy named Bud
She had a psychotic episode,
and drowned the newborn in the bathtub
Vroom, vroom/ No right to choose can still spell a baby's doom
Vroom, vroom/ Ashley's in jail/Her rapist won't be there
any time soon
That's quite enough/ Yes, it's time to suck/
Similar to a vacuum cleaner, the mega vac
Insert the hose/ You're aware of where it goes/
The power is turned all the way up to the max
Lay back, you'll be alright/ Try your best to relax
I'll extract that sucker directly out of it's amniotic sac
One, two, three, like so/ Here she blows!
See, that wasn't so hard/ Rest up,
I have ten more patients to go

Join me and dance, dance, the dance of death
Aborted fetuses will never draw a single breath
If complications during your pregnancy means
that you'll die
Politicians prefer it if you don't survive
Vroom, vroom, leads to the dance/
You bet, the dance of death
The government will sign your death warrant
by keeping you in check
This state and my ethics always seem to clash
Thanks to my trusty vacuum cleaner
I'll continue filling these trash bags

RELENTLESS REDRUM

My venacular is spectacular
when speaking of malevolence
Randolph is dead, just hid his body
without leaving any evidence
Due to sun exposure, I'll hastily dispose of Jill
but don't be obnoxious
The odor of her corpse decomposing
in my tub is guaranteed to make you nauseous
Guts spilled with earth shattering shrills/
Just asking to be eviscerated
The body will be properly disposed of/
I'd prefer not to be incarcerated
Hydrochloric acid will be utilized
to dissolve this woman's remains
Part of me wishes that I would get caught simply
to garner the fame
It's not fantasy or hyperbole to claim
that I'm a master cranium driller
Let's make a toast but not a mess
to a massive blood spiller
Aortas and severed arteries/
Mutilated loons and baffoons
Succumb to my egregious deviance/
Burial preference, mausoleum or tomb?
I'm dismissive of your fondness for feeding pigeons/
Not my kind of bird
I'll have vultures feast on your rotting flesh/

It's the least that you deserve
I'm anxious to taste your pancreas/
Makes me quiver to chew on your liver
Swallow pieces of salty appendix/
Anatomize your body, I must remember
I'm concerned that your open chest cavity, so sweet,
it'll give me cavities
Why do people fear me?/
A question that always baffles me
My liberating situation comes to fruition
with your strangulation
This darling should be dancing with the stars/
A serial killer sensation
Suffer seperation from the bladder/
Don't deprive me, I'm getting madder
No hesitation in providing castrations/
Subsequently, when you walk you'll probably stagger
Laugh hard, the joke's on you/
Bounces off rubber then sticks like glue
A broadsword thrusted through
Corey's belly causes sunlight to stream straight through
Committing murder,
I must deny if my freedom's at risk I'm flying high
Can't help taking pictures of Aaron bleeding
all over the couch/ He's a little camera shy
When in love I might elope/
Stick a pair of scissors in my wife's throat
Take her carcass on a cruise for our honeymoon,
then throw her off of the boat

Such tenacity for redrum/
It's in Bridget's best interest to run
I'm determined to club her like a seal/
Declare me public enemy number one
How many more can I possibly kill?/
Carnage has mass appeal
I refuse to stop doing what I do with due diligence/
Sooner or later I'll get my fill
Oh darn, FBI agents are in front of my house,
so I better sneak out the back
They didn't hesitate to open fire,
and stopped me dead in my tracks

THE COUGAR HUNTS
AT NIGHT

Everyone knows that Mindy Monroe
is a wealthy widow
All the glitter and fame
that remains isn't just for show
Back out on the dating market at age 53
Any man foolish enough to betray
her trust is predestined to bleed
Mindy prefers her suitors
to be much younger and well fit
Last year her twenty-nine year old boyfriend,
Benny had a little accident
After discovering her beau was a cheater,
and had several other women in the sack
Mindy became more focused
than ever to put the relationship back on track
by coming to terms with the current predicament,
and what their association lacked
Out of the kindness of Mindy's heart,
she arranged treatment for Benny's bad back
He had been suffering horrendous chronic pain
for over a year with difficulty to endure
Ms. Monroe arranged an appointment
for a more aggressive style of acupuncture
For this particular session Benny removed
most of his clothing prior to lying down

on the table while soothing whale songs played/
Oh, how he loved that sound
A scornful woman who wishes to excise
from her life all traces of evil
The acupuncturist owed Mindy a favor/
She utilized knives instead of needles
Of course it's not customary to incapacitate
a patient that's on the table
Restraints are in place in case Benny tried to escape/
He wouldn't actually be able
Relaxation here is the key/
The session was all paid for in cash
With a drawer full of knives,
the acupuncturist made each stab
wound deeper than the last
According to the coroner's report the death
was ruled accidental
Ms. Monroe having the monetary means
to pay off elected officials is merely coincidental
In the present day,
Trevor is the new man in Mindy's life
that she must expunge
Her new beau with humble beginnings has
forgotten his place while becoming quite the sponge
The other night Mindy caught Trevor
with a floozy which wasn't the least bit funny
An epiphany made it all so clear that
Mindy's beau was only interested in her money
Plans were made for Trevor to embark

on a trip to the islands/
There will be scuba diving
Unbeknownst to him, he may not return
with only a slim chance of surviving
Trevor attempted to take his lady
to the cleaners with a substantial
withdrawal from the bank
Before scuba diving, he failed to notice that 60%
of the oxygen had been removed from his tank
There he was in a tropical climate,
swimming under the sea
In no time at all the tank's air was depleted,
and Trevor struggled to breathe
The scuba diver swam far too deep/
While panicking, he almost swallowed his tongue
Reaching the surface was now a pipedream
as water filled his lungs
Ms. Monroe said, "I'll be damned
If I allow any man to manipulate me"
A week later, Trevor's body was recovered
from the ocean/ It was tightly bound in seaweed
Mindy has always presented herself as a sweetheart
but not all is what it seems
Heaven help any young man that encounters
this cougar while out on the dating scene

SWEET LULLABY 2

After two miscarriages,
Olivia gave birth to a stillborn baby
Fortune doesn't seem to follow this despondent,
broken hearted lady
Why is it that other women have been blessed
with children and not her?
Seems like a cruel joke, but that is what God prefers
Only a week passed since it happened/
Concealing all signs of grief
She's back working at the hospital
with the belief that thy Lord is a thief
A nurse that hid all hints of sadness
Olivia's colleagues were oblivious
of her descent into madness
If Olivia can't have a baby,
her desire was to take everyone else's away
She thought, "God should've allowed me to have mine/
This will make him pay"
Ms. Rodgers had recently given birth to Gigi/
Olivia snuck into her room
and saw the newborn baby wrapped
in a blanket like a cocoon
The nurse wished to provide her own brand
of help by sealing Ms. Rodgers' fate
A pillow placed over the face, easy to suffocate
Then she wrapped Gigi in her deceased
mother's coat with a vile

duty to do this in earnest
Olivia brought it down to the basement,
then placed the infant inside of the furnace
Well, that's that/ Turn up the thermostat
This baby is now sizzling/ Her first and final act
The murderer went upstairs to the nursery,
ready to raise the death toll
She stood towering over the bassinets with a heart so cold
So, why not play a game
that might be considered a little droll
with a wooden mallet in hand it's time for Whac-A-Mole
This woman unapologetically bashed
infants into ground round
Once the pounding finally stopped there
ceased to be a sound
A copious amount of newborns were still alive/
Please, stop your whining
Many of those who were on site suddenly started crying
Definitely the sound is deafening/
This and all the while
Olivia has a low tolerance and easily becomes volatile
Someone must help these children/
No, this is not a prank
The nurse is in possession of a carbon based steel tank
How on earth will it reach?/
It comes with a spray nozzle attached
Despite being quite heavy,
Olivia strapped the tank to her back
There aren't any more reasons to worry/

Now the problem has been solved
Fully loaded and ready to spray
with a container of ethanol
It was God that forced her hand
with a vision so violently lucid
Little reason to pray while the nurse sprays
a form of flammable fluid
Olivia is one hell of a woman,
certainly quite a catch
She left the ethanol behind and walked out,
but not before striking a match
These babies were burned alive
which can cause nausea like vertigo
Olivia's dizzy with her own version
of winning since the nursery became an inferno
Then the nurse decided to leave town
which seemed to be a safe bet
as a contingency in case one or two
of the parents might be upset

CLASS DISMISSED

Hello, my name is Marisol/
A clinically depressed sixteen year old girl
There are some mean girls that torment me,
so I'm mad at the world
Today I brought to school some artillery/
Where are my manners?/ That's just so rude of me
I'll introduce "Shotty" to individuals
who are destined to face some penalties
A 12 gauge shotgun in my arms,
cocked faster than a jack rabbit
Bullies are asking for it/
Now they're going to have it
Found Marissa in history class,
learning about Napoleon Bonaparte
If only he could bear witness to her head
and neck being blown apart
I have a score to settle/
We can sit back and do the math
Quite frankly it's wishful thinking/
There's no escape from my wrath
My counselor claimed that this is a safe haven
for all children on their behalf
There are more than a few faculty members
that'll be attending this blood bath
Kids hiding underneath desks, keep ducking,
not halfway done
Shit, I'm out of tampons/ Yeah, you better run

Lar Grimes and I had a date/
He drove me somewhere secluded to see the stars
I refused to "put out", so he put me out of his car
This is not the demeanor of a gentleman/
Today I spotted him in the gym
This is where life begins/My mistake, this is where it ends
In my possession are plethora of shotgun shells
I'll give Lar one for all the memories,
and another sends him to hell
In the name of posterity/ No, it's not charity
A favor is what has been given/
Imagine if he would've married me
While running through the cafeteria,
I caught that obnoxious lunch lady
Gave her a blast from the past/
Now she's lying in a bloody pool of gravy
This employee is guilty of serving burnt tater tots with
an attitude, which is an infraction
Watching her die slow provoked a wealth of satisfaction
Do you see how the tables have turned?
Tutors are required for the lessons
that haven't been learned
These goddamn bullies are bitches
that are profusely refusing to behave
When the 12 gauge is aimed at them
with ease I can persuade
These heifers to back off/ Trudy begged me to stop
As if I were a barber/
Don't worry, I'll take just a little off of the top

Then proceeded in blowing Trudy's brains out for
spreading rumors about me online
The janitor better call for back up,
or he'll be working overtime
Trudy's body turned cold like a town
that's been hit by a polar vortex
She lost her mind and said, goodbye,
to her cerebral cortex
Tabitha is the worst/ Calls me lame/
She's the main culprit to blame
A shotgun blast gave her a tummy ache/
It's hardly a shame that she's now slain
Then I finished off all of her allies/
Every single one deserved to be dead
Assumingly, the authorities are outside/
Time for one more act of bloodshed
After entering a vacant classroom,
I sat down feeling contentment and alone
Put the barrel of the shotgun in my mouth/
Mom and Dad, I'm never coming home... Click!

Sean Seville is an author/entertainer from Chicago, Illinois.